JAMESTOWN  PUBLISHERS

Themes *in* Reading

TEACHER'S GUIDE

JAMESTOWN PUBLISHERS
A DIVISION OF NTC/CONTEMPORARY
PUBLISHING COMPANY

Manufactured in the United States of America
International Standard Book Number: 0-89061-814-3
10 9 8 7 6 5 4 3 2 1

Executive Editor

Marilyn Cunningham

Editorial

Michael Carpenter

Paulinda Lynk

Production and Design

PiperStudiosInc

Contents

Introduction

Themes in Reading is a theme-based middle grades reading series. It includes three anthologies of high-quality literature—fiction, nonfiction, and poetry—by multicultural authors. The average readability level of each book is seventh grade. Instructional support for all three anthologies is provided in this teacher's guide.

The literature in the program centers on themes that are relevant to middle-grade students and that will help them develop critical reading and thinking skills.

The program is built around three major strands: reading strategies, reading comprehension skills, and author's craft skills. The teacher's guide lesson plan provides suggestions for direct instruction in each of these strands and makes explicit the connection between reading and writing.

Purposes

Themes in Reading focuses on the reading skills and strategies that make students engaged readers and improve their critical-thinking skills.

Some specific purposes of the program are as follows:

- to help students experience reading comprehension as a thinking process that has general application to reading outside the classroom

- to build students' confidence and self-esteem

- to introduce students to quality contemporary literature

- to make clear the connection between the experiences that authors write about and the students' own lives

- to encourage students to become independent readers by motivating them to seek out and read works by the same authors and by other authors they have heard about

- to provide good models for the students' own writing

Features

Each of the three student anthologies contains four theme-based units and twenty or more selections chosen for their quality and relevance to the students' everyday lives. It is especially important to note that the literature is

- unadapted

- unabridged

- contemporary

- multicultural

The selections and authors represent both genders and a variety of cultures. This diverse representation makes it possible for students to relate to the experiences of the authors and to note the universality of experiences among people of varying cultures.

The teacher's guide includes detailed lesson plans for each selection. Direct instruction and cooperative learning activities provide opportunities for the students to interact with the teacher and with each other.

The skills instruction is literature based. Strategies such as using prior knowledge, predicting, recalling information, and summarizing are part of the ongoing instruction. Reading comprehension skills help students understand the selection. Author's craft skills include techniques writers use to make selections interesting and relevant. Students are guided in transferring these skills to their own writing.

Using the Student Books

The student anthology includes many features that create interest and provide support for the student in reading and understanding the selections.

Unit Opener

Uses art and text on the unit opener spread to introduce the theme and provide opportunities for discussion.

Accomplishments

Accomplishments can be great or small. Winning a gold medal in the Olympics is an accomplishment. So is learning to play the piano well or making the baseball team or even getting your homework done on time.

Accomplishing something usually takes determination and hard work but makes people feel good about themselves. Think about an accomplishment you are proud of. What makes it so special?

In this unit you will read about people who succeeded in accomplishing their dreams or goals. In doing so, they gained a great deal of personal satisfaction and in some cases inspired others to work hard to reach their own goals.

As you read, think about your goals and dreams—those you had in the past and those you have now. Think about why they are important to you.

Art

Encourages students to discuss what they think each element of the illustration symbolizes and how it relates to the theme.

Text

Invites students to use prior knowledge to understand each theme and how it relates to their personal experiences. They discuss what the theme means to them, and they set goals for reading the selections in the unit.

Selection

Involves students in active reading of engaging fiction, nonfiction, and poetry.

Art

Helps students preview a selection and discuss how it might be connected to the theme.

Introduction

Helps students build background, suggests a purpose for reading a selection, and encourages students to set their own purposes for reading.

Vocabulary

Defines specialized and difficult vocabulary in the margin at point of use. Students may also keep their own lists of words they need to clarify and write a definition and a sentence for each word.

That Something Special: Dancing with the Repertory¹ Dance Company of Harlem

Leslie Rivera

Each of us has something we are good at. What does the poet think is special about herself?

¹ a collection of musical or theatrical works performed by a particular person or group

They tell me
that I have that something special.
But I don't see it the way they do.
That something
is what I give to them
my audience
and what I get back in return
is amazing.
I pour out my heart,
my soul, and every little dream
that I have.
People see it
and respond.
It is the sole reason I dance.

It is my way of reaching out
touching the world
letting it see my dreams and hopes.
It's that something special
that makes me give to my audiences
that makes them know what I feel.
And for them to see that
is an accomplishment all its own.

About the Author

Leslie Rivera was lucky enough to be chosen as one of twelve eighth-grade girls who took part in a special literature project in their New York neighborhood. The group met with authors and teachers who encouraged them to read and critique the works of writers with similar backgrounds and also to write and edit poetry and short stories about their own experiences. Their finished works were published in the book *Hispanic, Female and Young: An Anthology.*

16 Accomplishments   That Something Special 17

About the Author

Introduces the author. Students can discuss how the author's experiences relate to theirs and how knowing something about the author helps them understand the selection.

Responding Page

Relates back to the selection and to the unit theme. The Think Back questions reinforce comprehension of the selection. The Discuss and Write sections provide opportunities for cooperative learning and writing activities that are relevant to the selection and usually based on techniques the author used in the selection.

Theme Links

Makes connections between the selections, the unit theme, and students' own lives and experiences. At least two activities encourage cooperative learning. One activity—The Theme and You—calls for a personal response to the theme.

Responding to the Poem

▼ **Think Back**

Why does the speaker dance?

What is "that something special"?

What does the speaker say is the audience's accomplishment?

▼ **Discuss**

The speaker refers to dancing as a way to communicate to her audience. Do you agree with her? In what ways might a dancer communicate with an audience?

If you were Rivera, which would you be prouder of, your dancing abilities or your relationship with the audience? Which is a more satisfying accomplishment? Why?

▼ **Write**

Freewrite How do you share a skill, a talent, or a special interest with others? Write down every thought that comes into your head about what you do. Think about how your sharing makes you and others feel.

Write a Poem "That Something Special" is written in free verse. The poem seems to flow naturally from one idea to the next. Using the thoughts and ideas from your freewriting activity, write a poem about your special talent or interest.

Theme Links
Accomplishments

In this unit, you've read about people who succeeded in accomplishing their dreams or goals. You have also thought about your own goals and about what it means to feel proud of something you've done.

▼ **Group Discussion**

With a partner or in a small group, talk about the selections in the unit and how they relate to the theme and to your own lives. Use questions like the following to guide the discussion.
• What is special about each character or subject?
• How did their accomplishments affect others?
• Which accomplishment can you relate to?
• How would you define an accomplishment?

▼ **Meet the Characters**

Imagine that you are a person or character from one of the selections in this unit. You've been asked to give a short speech about yourself—what you do, why you do it, and what it means to you. Write your speech, practice at home, and then give your speech to the class.

▼ **Everyday Accomplishments**

Start a scrapbook about people who have accomplished something important to them or to others. You can include people you know, people you have heard or read about, or yourself. Your scrapbook might include any of the following.
• newspaper or magazine clippings
• drawings
• photos
• charts, maps
• notes, letters

For each entry, write a paragraph or two describing the accomplishment and commenting on why you think it was worthwhile.

▼ **The Theme and You**

What is special about you? Think of something you've accomplished or would like to accomplish. Write a letter to a relative or friend sharing your news. Explain what it took to do what you did and how it made you feel. Or write about something you would like to do in the future and why you would like to do it.

40 Accomplishments   Theme Links 41

Using the Teacher's Guide

Each one-page lesson plan serves as a step-by-step guide for direct instruction before, during, and after reading the selection.

Summary
Provides background information for the teacher.

Active Reading
Suggests different ways of reading the selection (silently, in groups, with a partner, and so on). Reading aloud activities familiarize students with important style elements of a selection such as dialogue, humor, and various types of emphasis. Encourages strategic reading by suggesting that students

- make predictions before and during reading and check their predictions periodically

- stop periodically to summarize and revise predictions on the basis of additional information

- stop to clarify unfamiliar vocabulary or concepts while reading

If necessary, students can refer back to the selection to answer the questions on the Responding page.

Reading Follow-up
Provides for discussion of the Think Back and Discuss sections on the Responding page.

Writing
Focuses on writing techniques and types of writing. Provides direct instruction in author's craft skills. Includes writing activities that link the selection, the theme, and the particular skill being studied.

Reading Comprehension
Direct instruction and activities focus on reading comprehension skills that help students interpret the selection. May include additional information about the author, the story, or a culture for deeper understanding and appreciation of the selection.

Beautiful Junk
Jon Madian

Story Summary

Charlie is a boy who lives in Los Angeles. He and his friends like to destroy old bottles, records, and other debris that litter the alleys of the city. One day Charlie meets an elderly man collecting the same type of objects that Charlie is destroying. Intrigued by the old man, Charlie follows him to his home and discovers that the old man has built three large towers and other structures out of the junk he collects.

Prereading

1. Start an art chart on the board by having students describe the different visual arts, such as painting, sculpture, and drawing. Next to each art, have students list the materials used by artists working in that medium.

2. Read the title on page 26 aloud. Ask students how junk can be beautiful. Then read the introduction and help students set a purpose for reading.

Active Reading

1. Invite a student to read the first two paragraphs aloud. Encourage students to predict what they think will happen and why.

2. Encourage students to read the story in small groups, with each group member preparing to read and then reading several paragraphs aloud. Stop at appropriate points to discuss what is happening or whenever a student has a clarification question. Remind students that they should summarize what they've read so far and predict what will happen next.

3. Have students read the questions on page 39 silently and think about the answers.

Reading Follow-up

Discuss the questions on page 39 with the class. Bring out the following concepts:

- Charlie finds the old man's interest in junk very strange.

- Charlie's curiosity gets the better of him. He is very interested in finding out what the old man does with all the junk he collects.

- At first, Charlie thought the old man was crazy because he collected junk. Once Charlie saw the old man's creation, his impression of him changed to admiration and respect.

Reading Comprehension

Compare and Contrast

Invite a volunteer to describe what Charlie is like at the beginning of the story. Then invite a student to describe Charlie at the end of the story. To help students gain a deeper understanding and appreciation of Charlie, create a compare and contrast chart on the board. On the left side of the chart, write students' descriptions of Charlie before he met the old man. On the right side, write their descriptions of Charlie after he met the old man. Remind students that comparing and contrasting characters or events will help them understand characters, situations, settings, and events more vividly and in more detail by seeing how they are similar or different or how they have changed.

Writing

Author's Craft: Characterization

Ask students to describe the personalities of Charlie and the old man. Point out that authors reveal character through actions, thoughts, speech (dialogue), and direct description.

Encourage students to locate passages in the story that reveal what Charlie and the old man are like. Explain that characters are not static and that events in a story often cause them to change or grow.

Have students focus on how to reveal character as they work on the writing activities on page 39.

8   Volume 1

Themes in Reading Skills

Reading Strategies	Volume 1	Volume 2	Volume 3
Generating Questions	4,5,27	45,46,50,52,59	68,88
Predicting	all lessons	all lessons	all lessons
Using Prior Knowledge	all lessons	all lessons	all lessons
Rereading	4,11,20,29,30	37,52,53,59	68,74,75,82, 83,84,88
Skimming	7,22,26	40,44,47	69,89,92
Reading Comprehension			
Author's Purpose	7		88
Cause and Effect	14,28	36,47,54,58,61	69,75
Sequence	7,27	61	69,70,90
Compare and Contrast	8,13,15,20, 21,23	36,40,45,50, 53,59,60	66,67,71,74, 78,83,84,85
Draw Conclusions	23,28	47	76
Fact and Opinion	28	47	
Make Inferences	11,15		81
Make Judgments	4,19,20,28	45,50,54,57,60,61	84
Main Idea and Details	all lessons	all lessons	all lessons
Personal Experience	all lessons	all lessons	all lessons
Recall Information	all lessons	all lessons	all lessons
Summarize	5,8,12,15,16, 21,27	43,44,53	67,78
Special Vocabulary	7	37,38,44,50,57	69,89
Author's Craft			
Characterization	8,12,26	46,51,61	71,76,78,91
Dialogue	5,13,22,26	43,50	75,76,85,89
Figurative Language	11	37,45,59,60	66,68,77,84,92
Flashback/Foreshadowing	29	58	71
Point of View	12,14	54	83
Theme	23	39,52	68,70,81,89
Imagery	15,20,21		66,74,77,81,82
Mood/Tone	22,26	40,43,53	67,70,82
Descriptive Language	4,21	37,39,46	81,82
Rhythm/Rhyme	30	57	77
Story Elements	26,27	39,52,54,58,61	70,71,81
Types of Writing	6,16,19,28,29	36,38,43,44,47	75,88,90,92

JAMESTOWN PUBLISHERS

Themes *in* *Reading*

VOLUME *1*

Marta Salinas

Langston Hughes

Tom Bodett

Toni Cade Bambara

Christy Brown

Sook Nyul Choi

Joseph Bruchac

Erma Bombeck

and others

A MULTICULTURAL COLLECTION

Contents

Unit 1: Accomplishments

Building Background

Discuss with the class what an accomplishment is. Encourage students to share their ideas. Record the ideas in a concept web like the one below.

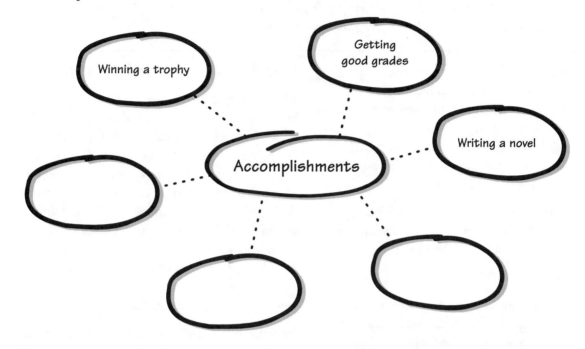

Previewing

Have students read and discuss the unit contents on page iv. Ask what kinds of selections they will be reading and how they think each selection relates to the theme.

Then discuss the illustration on pages 2 and 3. Ask what kind of accomplishment each part of the illustration represents. Add any new ideas to the concept web.

Reading and Discussion

Have students read the unit introduction silently. Call on volunteers to read each paragraph aloud. Use questions like the following to guide a discussion.

- How did this introduction change your ideas of what an accomplishment is?

- Who would like to share an accomplishment you are proud of? Why are you proud? What did it take to accomplish what you did?

Setting Theme Goals

Help students set their own goals for reading the selections and understanding the theme. Goals might include the following:

- to read about different kinds of accomplishments

- to appreciate the accomplishments of others

- to read interesting stories and poems

- to understand what accomplishments are and what it takes to accomplish something

Tell students to write at least two goals in their notebooks. Explain that they will refer to these goals after they have read the unit selections.

Yes, It Was My Grandmother

Luci Tapahonso

Poem Summary

A young woman describes with pride her free-spirited grandmother's talent for training horses. The speaker then talks about how similar she is to her grandmother.

Prereading

1. Ask the prereading questions below. Then prompt a discussion about students' grand-parents or other relatives.
   - *What do you know about your grandparents?*
   - *In what ways are you similar to one of your favorite grandparents or relatives?*

2. Choose a volunteer to read the introduction on page 4 aloud. Ask students to predict what the speaker's grandmother will be like.

Active Reading

1. Give students time to read the poem silently, or invite volunteers to read the poem aloud. If necessary, stop at appropriate points to discuss what they've read or to answer students' clarification questions.

2. Suggest that students read the poem a second time. Then have them read the questions on page 6 silently and think about the answers.

Reading Follow-up

Discuss the questions on page 6 with the class. Bring out the following concepts:

- The speaker's grandmother was a carefree and hardworking woman who had a talent for training horses. Unlike some people who prefer to work inside, she enjoyed the outdoors.

- The speaker admires her grandmother and takes pride in being her granddaughter. She describes how talented her grandmother was and then com-pares herself to her grandmother.

- Both the speaker and her grandmother are small, and their hair tangles often and is wild and untrained. Just like her grandmother, the speaker doesn't enjoy cooking.

Reading Comprehension

Make Judgments

Encourage students to share their opinions of the grandmother in "Yes, It Was My Grandmother." Ask what information they used to form their opin-ions. Point out that readers often make judgments about characters or events in a story or poem by deciding whether something is right or wrong, good or bad, or whether they would act like a certain char-acter. Making judgments requires using textual clues as well as personal values, experiences, tastes, and beliefs. Emphasize that valid judgments should be supported by logic, examples, facts, or experiences.

Encourage students to reexamine their judgments about the speaker's grandmother. Invite them to discuss whether their judgments are valid.

Writing

Author's Craft: Descriptive Language

Encourage volunteers to describe their mental images of the speaker's grandmother and to explain how they formed their images. Point out that good writers create strong, vivid images in readers' minds by using
- specific nouns
- action verbs
- interesting and precise adjectives

Ask students to find examples of descriptive lan-guage in the poem.

Suggest to students that they keep these points in mind as they work on the writing activities on page 6.

The Scholarship Jacket

M a r t a   S a l i n a s

Story Summary

Martha recalls when she was fourteen and about to graduate from the eighth grade. She expects to win a scholarship jacket, the award for having the highest grades for eight years. Then, because a teacher and the principal want to give the jacket to a student from a more influential family, they try to change the school's policy and charge $15.00 for the award. Martha is bitterly disappointed, but her grandfather helps her discover the true significance of winning an award for individual accomplishment.

Prereading

1. Ask these prereading questions. Then start a discussion about academic goals.
   - *What does the word* scholarship *mean to you?*
   - *Why is it important to do your best in school?*

2. Read the introduction on page 7 aloud. Discuss what students think the story will be about, and help them set a purpose for reading.

Active Reading

1. Call on volunteers to read the first two paragraphs aloud. Ask students to predict what they think will happen and why.

2. Have students read the story silently in small groups, stopping at appropriate points or whenever a student has a clarification question, to discuss what is happening. Students should summarize what they've read so far and predict what will happen next.

3. Have students read the questions on page 15 silently and think about the answers.

Reading Follow-up

Discuss the questions on page 15 with the class. Bring out the following concepts:

- Martha values the jacket because it is a reward for working hard, because her sister had won the jacket before her, and because it is her only chance to win a school-related prize.

- Mr. Boone wants to give the jacket to Joann because he feels that her father is more important than Martha's family.

- Martha's grandfather refuses to pay for the jacket because it represents personal achievement—something that can't be bought.

Reading Comprehension

Predict Outcomes

Call on students to predict something that might happen tomorrow. Ask what information they used to make each prediction. Explain that making predictions will help them understand what they read and that predictions should be based on story information and their own experiences.

Discuss predictions students made after reading the first two paragraphs of "The Scholarship Jacket." Then ask what predictions they made after reading through the third paragraph on page 10. What details led to these predictions?

Continue through other parts of the story, pointing out how predictions change as the reader learns new information.

Writing

Author's Craft: Dialogue

Remind students that dialogue is the conversation of characters in a story. Writers use dialogue to move the story along, to reveal information, and to show the thoughts and feelings of characters.

Have students find examples of dialogue in the story and explain what each example reveals.

Remind them to use quotation marks before and after each character's exact words as they work on the writing activities on page 15.

That Something Special:
Dancing with the Repertory Dance Company of Harlem

Leslie Rivera

Poem Summary

The speaker of this poem disagrees with those who tell her that her dancing talent is an accomplishment on its own. She says she dances to touch the world and to let others see and know what she feels: her relationship with her audience is the special accomplishment.

Prereading

1. Ask students to describe their favorite dancers or dances. Then create a cluster diagram with *dancing* at the center. Ask volunteers to put images and words in the outer circles to describe qualities that make dancing a unique art.

2. Invite a student to read the introduction on page 16 aloud. Encourage students to talk about what they think the poem will be about.

Active Reading

1. Read the poem aloud as the students follow along. Then ask volunteers to read the poem aloud, emphasizing the emotions and feelings it conveys.

2. Have students read the questions on page 18 silently and think about the answers.

Reading Follow-up

Discuss the questions on page 18 with the class. Elicit the following concepts:

- The speaker dances because she can express to the world her dreams and hopes as well as allow people to respond to her dancing.

- The "something special" is the special relationship between artist and audience—the giving of a special talent and the feeling the artist gets from the audience in return.

- The audience's accomplishment is being able to know what the dancer is feeling.

Reading Comprehension

Paraphrase

Invite volunteers to explain the meaning of "That Something Special." Point out that a paraphrase is a restatement of the ideas and details of a piece of writing in one's own words. Explain to students that when paraphrasing a poem, they should restate its ideas in prose.

Writing

Author's Craft: Free Verse

Unlike many poems that rhyme and are divided into stanzas, "That Something Special" does not seem to have any form. Remind students that this poem is written in free verse. Point out that free verse is poetry that does not follow the traditional poetic conventions of meter, rhyme, and stanza. In free verse, ideas are more important than structure. Poets who write free verse often experiment with natural rhythms of speech and the free flow of thoughts and feelings.

Have students keep these points in mind as they practice writing poetry in the writing activities on page 18.

The Contest
Janet Stevenson

Story Summary

With her coach's encouragement and confidence, Marian Anderson competes for the honor of singing at Lewisohn Stadium. After passing the first audition, Marian feels a pain in one ear, creating not only physical discomfort but also concern about whether she'd ever sing again. Despite the earache, Marian sings brilliantly in the semifinals, and the judges cancel the finals and award the Lewisohn Stadium appearance to Marian.

Prereading

1. Ask the prereading questions below. Then encourage students to start a list of contests they are familiar with. For each entry, have the students describe what the contestants compete for and how the winner is decided.

    - *In what ways do coaches or mentors help prepare contestants for competition?*
    - *What feelings and emotions do you associate with contests?*

2. Read the introduction on page 19 aloud. Discuss what students think the story will be about, and help them set a purpose for reading.

Active Reading

1. Invite volunteers to read the first two paragraphs aloud. Encourage students to predict what they think will happen and why. Write their predictions on the chalkboard.

2. Have students skim the selection to find unfamiliar musical terms. Define the unfamiliar words and phrases so that students can continue reading the selection silently.

3. Have students read the questions on page 25 silently and think about the answers.

Reading Follow-up

Discuss the questions on page 25 with the class. Bring out the following concepts:

- Marian competed against three hundred contestants in the first round of the contest and sixteen in the semifinals.

- Marian had to sing with a painful abscess growing in her ear.

- Marian was so concerned about the pain in her ear that she wondered if she'd ever sing again.

Reading Comprehension

Author's Purpose

Encourage volunteers to suggest reasons why Janet Stevenson wrote "The Contest." Have students explain their opinions. Point out that writers write

- to entertain
- to inform
- to persuade

An author's purpose for writing often determines a reader's purpose. For example, if the author's purpose is to inform, then the reader sets a purpose to find out the information the author is presenting.

Ask volunteers to describe how they determined Janet Stevenson's purpose in writing "The Contest" and, therefore, their purposes for reading the selection. If necessary, point out that this selection is a biography of Marian Anderson and was written to inform readers about her life.

Writing

Author's Craft: Chronological Order

Remind students that when they write about a series of events, it is helpful for them and their readers to describe the events in chronological order—the order in which they happened.

Ask students to list events in "The Contest" in order. Remind students that words such as *first, second, next, before, after, then,* and *finally* are signal words that help readers understand the order of events. Remind students to use transition words as they work on the writing activities on page 25.

Beautiful Junk
A Story of the Watts Towers
Jon Madian

Story Summary

Charlie is a boy who lives in Los Angeles. He and his friends like to destroy old bottles, records, and other debris that litter the alleys of the city. One day Charlie meets an elderly man collecting the same type of objects that Charlie is destroying. Intrigued by the old man, Charlie follows him to his home and discovers that the old man has built three large towers and other structures out of the junk he collects.

Prereading

1. Start an art chart on the board by having students describe the different visual arts, such as painting, sculpture, and drawing. Next to each art, have students list the materials used by artists working in that medium.

2. Read the title on page 26 aloud. Ask students how junk can be beautiful. Then read the introduction and help students set a purpose for reading.

Active Reading

1. Invite a student to read the first two paragraphs aloud. Encourage students to predict what they think will happen and why.

2. Encourage students to read the story in small groups, with each group member preparing to read and then reading several paragraphs aloud. Stop at appropriate points to discuss what is happening or whenever a student has a clarification question. Remind students that they should summarize what they've read so far and predict what will happen next.

3. Have students read the questions on page 39 silently and think about the answers.

Reading Follow-up

Discuss the questions on page 39 with the class. Bring out the following concepts:

• Charlie finds the old man's interest in junk very strange.

• Charlie's curiosity gets the better of him. He is very interested in finding out what the old man does with all the junk he collects.

• At first, Charlie thinks the old man is crazy because he collects junk. Once Charlie sees the old man's creation, his impression of him changes to admiration and respect.

Reading Comprehension

Compare and Contrast

Invite a volunteer to describe what Charlie is like at the beginning of the story. Then invite a student to describe Charlie at the end of the story. To help students gain a deeper understanding and appreciation of Charlie, create a compare and contrast chart on the board. On the left side of the chart, write students' descriptions of Charlie before he met the old man. On the right side, write their descriptions of Charlie after he met the old man. Remind students that comparing and contrasting characters or events will help them understand characters, situations, settings, and events more vividly and in more detail by seeing how they are similar or different or how they have changed.

Writing

Author's Craft: Characterization

Ask students to describe the personalities of Charlie and the old man. Point out that authors reveal character through actions, thoughts, speech (dialogue), and direct description.

Encourage students to locate passages in the story that reveal what Charlie and the old man are like. Explain that characters are not static and that events in a story often cause them to change or grow.

Have students focus on how to reveal character as they work on the writing activities on page 39.

Theme Links: Accomplishments

Using the Theme Links

Explain to the class that the activities on this page will help them make connections between the selections they have just read and discussed and their own lives.

Every student should participate in a group discussion of the theme and complete the The Theme and You activity. Let students choose one of the remaining Theme Link activities or suggest another activity they would like to work on independently or with a partner or group.

Student Activities

Group Discussion
Encourage participants to list additional questions or concepts they would like to discuss. Allow fifteen to twenty minutes for the discussions. Then have groups share their observations with the class.

Meet the Characters
Students can practice their speeches at home with parents or family members as the audience. Tell them to ask for feedback from the audience to help them make their speeches accurate and interesting.

Everyday Accomplishments
You may wish to make this an ongoing class activity, with all students contributing to the scrapbook as they find information or think of an accomplishment worth noting.

The Theme and You
Help students to understand that there is something "special" about each of them and to identify what that something is. Encourage students to share their writing with the class, but only if they wish to do so.

Checking Theme Goals

Have students refer to the goals they set at the beginning of this unit. Discuss their goals and outcomes with the class. Ask what they might add to the concept web they worked on before reading the unit.

Unit 2: Acts of Kindness

Building Background

Discuss with the class how people respond to kindness. Encourage students to describe times when someone was particularly kind to them. Invite them to talk about how they felt. Record their ideas on a chart like the one at the right.

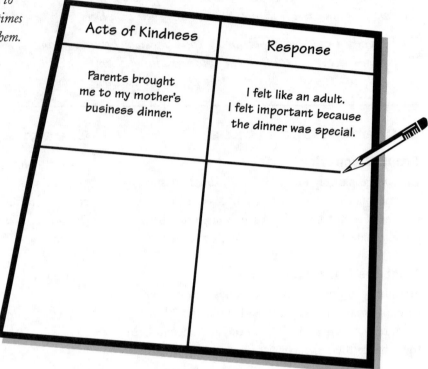

Acts of Kindness	Response
Parents brought me to my mother's business dinner.	I felt like an adult. I felt important because the dinner was special.

Previewing

Have students read and discuss the unit contents on page v. Encourage them to talk about the kinds of selections they will be reading and how they think each selection might relate to the theme.

Discuss the illustration on pages 42 and 43. Ask students what act of kindness each part of the illustration depicts. Add any new ideas to the idea chart.

Reading and Discussion

Have students read the unit introduction silently and think about answers to the questions. Then invite volunteers to read each paragraph aloud. Use questions like the following to help guide the discussion.

- How did this introduction change your ideas of what kindness is and how you treat people?

- What are the rewards for being kind and thoughtful? How does it make you feel to make someone else feel good?

Setting Theme Goals

Help students set their own goals for reading the selections and understanding the theme. Goals might include the following:

- to read about ways in which people are kind

- to read interesting stories and poems

- to learn from and be inspired by the kindness of others

Tell students to write at least two goals in their notebooks. Remind them that they will refer to these goals after they have read the unit selections.

Oranges
Gary Soto

Poem Summary

The speaker recalls his first date, when he and the girl went to a drugstore to buy candy. With only a nickel and two oranges in his pocket, he doesn't say anything when his date picks a ten-cent candy. He places a nickel and an orange on the counter. The store clerk accepts the orange as payment, knowing that the speaker doesn't have ten cents and not wanting to embarrass the boy in front of his date.

Prereading

1. Ask the prereading questions below. Then invite students to talk about dates, crushes, or boyfriends and girlfriends.
   - *What makes a date a "date"?*
   - *Where do young people go on dates?*

2. Invite a student to read the introduction on page 44 aloud. Ask students to predict what the poem will be about.

Active Reading

1. Have students read the poem silently. Then ask several students to take turns reading sections of the poem aloud. Discuss the poem and answer students' clarification questions after the oral reading.

2. Before students read and think about answers to the questions on page 47, suggest that they read the poem a second time silently.

Reading Follow-up

Discuss the questions on page 47 with the class. Bring out the following concepts:

- The speaker has a crush on the girl. One can tell by his descriptions of her, the fact that he let her buy a ten-cent candy when he only had a nickel, and because they held hands as they walked.

- The speaker pays for the candy with a nickel and an orange.

- The speaker and the store clerk communicate by eye contact. The clerk realizes that the speaker doesn't have enough money for the chocolate, but accepts the orange as payment so as not to embarrass the boy.

Reading Comprehension

Make Inferences

Invite students to tell how the speaker feels after leaving the drugstore or to describe why the store clerk accepted the orange as payment. Remind students that authors, especially poets, often do not state ideas directly in a text. They leave it to the reader to fill in the information they leave out— to make inferences. The reader does this by combining clues in the story with knowledge from his or her own experiences.

Encourage volunteers to explain how they determined the speaker's feelings and why the clerk acted as she did.

Invite students to read the poem again and to make an inference about the girl's feelings. Ask them to explain what clues helped them make the inference.

Writing

Author's Craft
Figurative Language: Similes

Remind students that a simile is a direct comparison in which one thing is said to be like something else. A simile uses the word *like* or *as*.

Ask students to find the similes in the poem and to explain the comparisons. Encourage students to be creative as they develop similes for the writing activities on page 47.

Andrew

B e r r y   M o r g a n

Story Summary

Roxie tells about the time she took Andrew, a newborn, from his young and incompetent parents, offer-
ing to take care of him until he was "good and strong." Roxie's hopes of raising the child are dashed when
the sheriff returns the infant to his family. In relating the incident, Roxie reveals much about her life.
She is single, childless, and has lived alone since her mother died. When her mother was ill, Roxie took
care of her. Andrew was her way of filling the void left by her mother's death.

Prereading

1. Ask the prereading questions below. Then start a discussion about helping other people.
   - *Have you ever had to make sacrifices for the people you love? What were the sacrifices?*
   - *Why do you make sacrifices for the people you care about?*

2. Read the introduction on page 48 aloud. What do students think the story will be about? Help them set a purpose for reading.

Active Reading

1. Call on volunteers to read the first two paragraphs aloud. On the board, write the name *Roxie*. Invite students to give short descriptions of Roxie, based on the first two paragraphs. Have students predict what they think might happen to Roxie.

2. Have students read the story silently. Alert them to stop for clarification if they do not understand the rural southern expressions. Interrupt periodically for students to summarize the story to a particular point in the text.

3. Have students read the questions on page 57 silently and think about the answers.

Reading Follow-up

Discuss the questions on page 57 with the class. Bring out the following concepts:

- Roxie was going to the home of a white lady who had hired her to help set ducks.

- Andrew's mother is the granddaughter of Mrs. Littell, a woman who lives in the community. His father is a soldier.

- Roxie thinks that Andrew's mother can't take care of him because she created a hazard when she built a fire on the floor on a piece of tin, and she did not have water or milk for Andrew.

Reading Comprehension

Summarize

Ask a volunteer to summarize "Andrew" and then explain how he or she decided which information to include in the summary. Explain that a summary is a short way of telling what a story is about. It includes the most important information—the characters, set-ting, events, and problems—and helps readers keep track of the plot. Discuss the summaries students gave while reading "Andrew." Were they helpful?

Writing

Author's Craft: Point of View

Invite a volunteer to define point of view. If neces-sary, remind students that point of view is the per-spective from which a story is told. There are two main points of view:

- first-person point of view: A main character is also the narrator, using the personal pronouns *I* and *me*.
- third-person point of view: The narrator is some-one "outside the story," using the personal pro-nouns *he, she,* and *they*.

Ask students to locate parts of "Andrew" that reveal the point of view. Point out that sometimes the author enters the viewpoints of several characters. This is called third-person omniscient point of view. Have students remember who the narrator is as they work on the writing activities on page 57.

Thank You, M'am
Langston Hughes

Story Summary

Instead of grabbing the purse and making a quick getaway, Roger falls and is swiftly apprehended by Mrs. Luella Bates Washington Jones, owner of the purse. Mrs. Jones wants to make an impression on the boy that he will never forget, so she takes Roger to her home. Once there, she cleans and feeds him and gives the boy ten dollars. Her anger is replaced by kindness and compassion.

Prereading

1. Invite students who have been victims of crime or who know of somebody who has to describe how they felt about it. Make a Problem/Solution chart about crime in the United States. Have students describe and record problems that crime creates. Then have students give solutions to the problems. Encourage students to return to this chart after they've read "Thank You, M'am" to add or delete anything.

2. Invite a student to read the title and introduction on page 58 aloud. Then discuss what students think the story will be about.

Active Reading

1. Give students time to read the story silently.

2. Have students read the questions on page 64 silently and think about the answers.

Reading Follow-up

Discuss the questions on page 64 with the class. Bring out the following concepts:

- Luella Jones is not afraid of Roger. She kicks him in the seat of his pants, pulls him up by the shirt front, and takes him to her home.

- Roger wanted to buy a pair of blue suede shoes with the stolen money.

- Luella Jones treats Roger very kindly. At first she wants to punish the boy, but her anger turns to compassion when she finds out that there's nobody home at his house. She then instructs him to clean up while she prepares a meal for him. Finally, she gives him ten dollars to buy the blue suede shoes.

Reading Comprehension

Compare and Contrast

Explain to students that authors often juxtapose two or more things, persons, events, or stories in order to emphasize similarities and differences in those things. Learning how to compare and contrast will lead to a greater understanding of a story.

Remind students that when they compare, they look for similarities; when they contrast, they look for differences.

Have students identify how Roger and Luella Jones are alike and different. Write their observations on the board. Then have students explain how the characters change in the story.

Writing

Author's Craft: Dialogue

Remind students that dialogue helps
- move the story along
- reveal information
- show the thoughts and feelings of characters

Have students look through "Thank You, M'am" and discuss what information is revealed through dialogue and how that information moves the story along.

Remind students to use quotation marks before and after each character's exact words as they work on the writing activities on page 64.

Coming Home
A Dog's True Story
Ted Harriott

Story Summary

Bodger, a dog, tells this story about his life with his first master and the family that later adopts him. Bodger's first master, Paddy, was a beggar. Bodger helped Paddy get food by performing tricks and sniffing through garbage cans. When Paddy dies, Bodger is taken to a shelter. Finally, a woman whom Paddy and Bodger saw on their walks takes Bodger home to live with her. The dog shows his appreciation by bringing her and her husband a present: a smelly old lump of cheese.

Prereading

1. Invite students to talk about their pets. Then create a Pet Owner's Responsibility chart.

2. Read the introduction on page 65 aloud. Discuss with students how animals do communicate. What do they think the dog might say? Help them set a goal for reading.

Active Reading

1. Ask a student to read the first two paragraphs aloud. Encourage students to predict what they think will happen and why.

2. Allow students time to read the story silently or to prepare for and take parts to read it orally in small groups. Encourage students to read the narrator's—Bodger's—lines in an interesting style and to pay particular attention to Bodger's feelings and his reaction to the kindness shown to him.

3. Have students read the questions on page 69 silently and think about the answers.

Reading Follow-up

Discuss the questions on page 69 with the class. Bring out the following concepts:

- Paddy was an unemployed old man who spent the days walking the streets, begging and searching for food. Paddy cared deeply for Bodger and looked out for him until he died.

- Bodger shows that he likes his new masters by bringing them a gift.

- Paddy showed kindness by taking care of Bodger. Pub patrons were kind to Paddy and Bodger by giving them food and drinks. The woman shows kindness by adopting Bodger.

Reading Comprehension

Cause and Effect

Ask a volunteer to define a cause and effect relationship. Remind students that a cause is an event or action that directly results in another event or action—the effect. Students will be better readers if they recognize that specific events, actions, and character motives cause other events and actions.

Ask volunteers to explain the causes of each effect listed below:
- Paddy and Bodger walked the streets each day.
- Paddy held Bodger on his bed.
- The woman adopted Bodger.

Writing

Author's Craft: Point of View

Point of view is the perspective from which a story is told. Let students identify the point of view in "Coming Home." Have a student define these terms:
- first-person point of view (A main character narrates, using the personal pronouns *I* and *me*.)
- third-person point of view (The story is narrated by someone "outside the story," using the personal pronouns *he, she*, and *they*.)
- third-person omniscient point of view (The author enters the viewpoints of several characters at random.)

Encourage students to discuss how "Coming Home" would be different if it were told from the point of view of another character.

Birdfoot's Grampa

Joseph Bruchac

Poem Summary

The speaker of this poem describes a nighttime drive with an old man who is intent upon helping small toads cross the road. Oblivious to the rain, the wet grass, and their schedule, the old man shows kindness by helping the animals travel safely.

Prereading

1. Ask the prereading questions below. Then start a discussion about animal-rights groups and their goals.
   - *What roles do animals play in your lives?*
   - *Why do many people place less value on the lives of animals than on the lives of humans?*

2. Invite a volunteer to read the poem title and the introduction on page 70 aloud. Discuss what students think the poem will be about.

Active Reading

1. Give students time to read the poem silently. Then read the poem aloud in a cooperative reading. Have students organize into groups of three. Assign roles of narrator and actors. While the narrator reads the poem, the two actors perform the actions being described.

2. Have students read the questions on page 72 silently and think about the answers. You may also ask students to compare and contrast the way the old man treats the toads and the way humans treated Bodger in "Coming Home."

Reading Follow-up

Discuss the questions on page 72 with the class. Bring out the following concepts:

- The old man stops the car in order to help the small toads cross the road.

- The speaker says that the old man can't save all the toads and that the old man should accept that fact and move on.

- The old man is patient; he willingly stops the car many times. He is also concerned about the fate of the toads and is willing to put up with physical discomfort in order to help them.

Reading Comprehension

Understanding Native American Culture

Poet Joseph Bruchac is part Abenaki Indian. Like most North American Indians, the Abenaki respect the animals that they share the earth with. Many American Indians believe that all things on earth are connected; whatever happens to the animals will also happen to humans. This might explain why the old man is so concerned with the fate of the small toads.

Writing

Author's Craft: Imagery

Remind students that effective imagery is created by using descriptive details that appeal to one or more of the five senses. Vivid imagery creates mental images—words that evoke our memories of events and objects.

Initiate a discussion about how the images might change if the poem described a desert scene in the daytime or if it took place in another setting.

Grandma Hattie

Tom Bodett

Selection Summary

Tom Bodett relates a story that illustrates the kindness and compassion his Grandma Hattie showed to hoboes who traveled through the Midwest during the Depression. One Sunday during Christmas time, a storm washed away the little X the hoboes had written on a gatepost to let other hoboes know that this was a place where they could get a handout. Several days later, while a blizzard raged, Hattie noticed that the hoboes were not stopping. Braving the blizzard, Hattie went outside and wrote a big X on the gatepost. Bodett thinks of this story to help him remember the true meaning of charity.

Prereading

1. Ask the prereading questions below. Then start a discussion about charities.
    - *Is it important to help those who are less fortunate than you?*
    - *Which charities do you support?*

    Start a chart on the board that lists the various ways in which students can help those people who are less fortunate. Have students describe how these ways will help and how they can bring the actions about.

2. Read the introduction on page 73 aloud and explain that one way that Grandma Hattie is special is that she is generous. Discuss how students think she will show her generosity. Then help them set a purpose for reading.

Active Reading

1. Give students time to read the selection silently. If necessary, stop at appropriate points to discuss what is happening or whenever a student has a clarification question.

2. Remind students that they should summarize what they've read so far. Have students read the questions on page 77 silently and think about the answers.

Reading Follow-up

Discuss the questions on page 77 with the class. Bring out the following concepts:

- Grandma Hattie shows kindness by sending money and cards to family members on special occasions. During the Depression, she went out of her way to feed hoboes.

- Hattie sends cards and "newsy" letters that describe the weather and other topics.

- Bodett doesn't want to return the second five-dollar bill to Grandma Hattie because he's afraid it would embarrass her.

Reading Comprehension

Background Information

Students may not be familiar with the Great Depression and the effects it had on American citizens. Explain that the Great Depression (1929–1939) was a time of great economic despair. Although the Depression began in the United States, it soon became an international problem. In the United States, thousands of banks and financial institutions were forced to close. Between twelve and fifteen million workers were unemployed. Many of the unemployed wandered the country looking for work.

Writing

Author's Craft: Anecdotes/Incidents

Remind students that an anecdote is a story within a story that illustrates a point or tells what a character or person is like.

Have students explain what they would say about one of their relatives if they were to write an anecdote about that person. Invite students to describe the details they would use.

Have students keep the purpose of an anecdote in mind as they work on the writing activities on page 77.

Theme Links: Acts of Kindness

Using the Theme Links

The activities on these pages will help students make connections between the selections they have just read and discussed and their own lives.

Have all students participate in a group discussion of the theme and complete the The Theme and You activity. Students may choose one of the remaining Theme Link activities, or they may suggest another activity they would like to work on independently or with a partner or group.

Student Activities

Group Discussion

Encourage group members to list additional questions or concepts they would like to discuss. Allow fifteen to twenty minutes for the discussions. Then have groups share their observations with the class.

Hearing from the Characters

Have students review the selections and choose one on which to base their notes. Suggest that they practice their presentation several times with their partner before performing it for the class or video-taping it.

Everyday Acts of Kindness

Students may enjoy making this an ongoing class activity, with students nominating worthy recipients for the award on a regular basis.

The Theme and You

Help students understand that there are many opportunities to perform acts of kindness every day. Invite volunteers to share their writing with the class.

Checking Theme Goals

Have students refer to the goals they set at the beginning of this unit. Discuss their goals and outcomes with the class. Ask what they might add to the idea chart they worked on before reading the unit.

Unit 3: Communication

Building Background

Start a class discussion about what it means to communicate with others. Ask students to list as many ways of communicating as they can think of. Discuss the ways they have used.

Draw a chart like the one at the right on the chalkboard. List some communication situations like those shown. Ask students to name the methods of communication that can be used in each situation. Expand the chart by having students add their own communication situations and telling how best to accomplish them.

Communication	Methods
– conversation with boyfriend or girlfriend	– face-to-face talking; telephone
– news about the birth of a relative	– card or letter; telephone; Email
–	
–	

Previewing

Have students read and discuss the unit contents on page vi. Discuss the kinds of selections they will be reading and how they think each selection might relate to the theme.

Then discuss the illustration on pages 80 and 81. Ask students to identify each method of communication represented in the illustration. Add any new ideas to the chart.

Reading and Discussion

Have students read the unit introduction silently and think about how they would answer the questions. Then invite volunteers to read each paragraph aloud. Questions like the following will help guide a discussion.

* How did this introduction change your ideas about what it means to communicate?

* Who would like to share some examples of times when you communicated well with someone else or times when you just didn't seem to be able to make someone listen to you or get your point?

Setting Theme Goals

Help students set their own goals for reading the selections and understanding the theme. Goals might include the following:

* to read about different kinds of communication

* to see what happens when communication breaks down

* to read interesting stories and poems

* to understand why it's important to communicate with others

Tell students to write at least two goals in their notebooks. Remind them that they will refer to these goals after they have read the unit selections.

Letter for Sookan

Sook Nyul Choi

Story Summary

Before studying for a college history test, Sookan thinks about her family in Korea. She then reads a letter from her mother, who describes what is happening back home in Korea. Her mother's gentle encouragement and faith comfort Sookan and illustrate the power of written communications.

Prereading

1. Invite students to talk about times they've been away from their families. Then ask the following questions:
   - *What do you miss the most when you are away from your families?*
   - *What do you do to relieve the loneliness?*

2. Have a student read the introduction on page 82 aloud. What do students think the letter will say? Help students set a purpose for reading.

Active Reading

1. Invite a volunteer to read the first two paragraphs aloud. Encourage students to predict what they think will happen and why.

2. Allow students time to read the story silently. Stop at appropriate points to summarize what they've read so far and predict what will happen next. If necessary, stop whenever a student has a clarification question.

3. Have students read the questions on page 87 silently and think about the answers.

Reading Follow-up

Discuss the questions on page 87 with the class. Elicit the following concepts:

- Although Sookan's mother is concerned about Sookan and misses her, she knows that her daughter will succeed in college. Her brothers also miss her but are reluctant to write to her because they do not have money to send.

- Sookan feels deep love and respect for her mother. She also feels lonely being so far away from her home and guilty for not being there to help. Her feelings of melancholy give way to comfort and determination to do well in school to make her mother proud of her.

- Sookan's mother is a very proud and strong woman. She stresses the importance of maintaining family ties and of helping those who are less fortunate.

Reading Comprehension

Make Judgments

What do students think of Sookan and her mother? Why? Remind students that when they make judgments about characters or events in a story, they use details from the story as well as personal values, experiences, and beliefs.

Making judgments about characters in a story can help them connect with the literature. Encourage students to suggest advice either to Sookan or to her mother about how to relieve her loneliness.

Writing

Postcards

Invite students to describe postcards they have written or received. What kind of information is usually written on them? Point out that postcards are written to a specific person—or audience. Postcards are also written in informal language, similar to that used in a conversation. Most people usually write whatever comes to mind at that moment, often making a brief reference to the picture, art, or photograph that appears on the front of the postcard.

Remind students to keep a conversational tone as they work on the writing activities on page 87.

The Telephone

Edward Field

Poem Summary

The speaker of the poem says that his happiness depends on an "electric appliance"—the telephone. In an impersonal world the telephone brings "the human voice and the good news of friends."

Prereading

1. Start a discussion by describing your attitude toward telephone calls. Explain how you react when the telephone rings while you are busy. Then ask the following questions:
   - *When your phone rings, how do you react?*
   - *Do you get annoyed, or do you welcome the calls?*
   - *How often do you talk on the telephone?*

2. Use the questions in the introduction on page 88 to survey students on their attitudes toward the telephone. What attitude do they predict the speaker in the poem will have?

Active Reading

1. Give students time to read the poem silently. After reading the poem a first time, students might enjoy reading it aloud, emphasizing the emotions and feelings evident in the poem.

2. Have students read the questions on page 90 silently and think about the answers.

Reading Follow-up

Discuss the questions on page 90 with the class. Bring out the following concepts:

- The speaker lives in a large city. As an urbanite, the speaker is separated from friends.

- The speaker feels joyous at the thought that he is "in the world and wanted."

- Like a bear in winter, the speaker was hibernating—isolated from the world.

Reading Comprehension

Personal Experience

Invite students to describe their thoughts and feelings about talking on the telephone. Point out that the telephone is something that practically everybody has used. One way to better understand and appreciate the poem is to recall their own experiences with telephones. Students can ask themselves these questions:

- How are my experiences similar to or different from the speaker's?
- Based on my experiences, does the speaker discuss valid concerns or ideas?
- What do my experiences add to my understanding of the poem?

You might read the poem again, encouraging students to point out passages that remind them of their personal experiences.

Writing

Poet's Craft: Imagery

Imagery is created by using descriptive details that appeal to one or more of the five senses. In this poem, the poet creates contrasting images: emotional or physical coldness and emotional or physical warmth. Ask students to find images that fit each category.

coldness
- "separated from friends / By a tangle of subways"
- "I was . . . a bear in a cave / Drowsing through a shadowy winter"

warmth
- "It rings and I am alerted to love"
- "It rings and spring has come"
- "I . . . amble out into the sunshine"

The contrasting images express the speaker's mood before and after receiving phone calls.

Brainstorm images students might use in the writing activities on page 90.

The Letter "A"

C h r i s t y   B r o w n

Selection Summary

Paralyzed since birth by cerebral palsy, Christy Brown describes how, at age five, his life changed. While watching his sister practice writing letters, Christy suddenly seizes a piece of chalk in the toes of his left foot. After several attempts, Christy writes the letter A as his stunned family watches.

Prereading

1. Ask the prereading questions below. Then start a discussion about disabilities.
   - *In what ways do citizens with disabilities contribute to society?*
   - *How can you and your classmates help citizens with disabilities lead productive lives?*

2. Read the introduction on page 91 aloud. Students may not know what cerebral palsy is. Explain that cerebral palsy is the inability to control one's movement and speech, caused by damage to the brain before or during birth.

Active Reading

1. Call on volunteers to read the first two paragraphs aloud. Invite students to predict what they think will happen.

2. Allow students time to read the selection silently. Remind them to summarize every few paragraphs and predict what will happen next.

3. Have students read questions on page 97 silently and think about the answers.

Reading Follow-up

Discuss the questions on page 97 with the class. Bring out the following concepts:

- Until Christy learns to write, he is unable to communicate. He can't do anything by himself, and he is lonely.

- Christy's family is shocked at his sudden attempts to write. They stare at him and lean closer, making eye contact that encourages him to try harder.

- Christy could feel the tenseness and sense profound stillness in the room. He could hear the sound of the water tap, the ticking of the clock, and the soft hiss and crackle of fire logs.

Reading Comprehension

Compare and Contrast

Point out that Christy Brown describes two lives in "The Letter 'A'": his life before he learned to communicate and his life after. Remind students that comparing and contrasting things helps readers understand characters, situations, settings, and events more vividly and in more detail by seeing how they are similar or different. To help students gain a deeper understanding and appreciation of Christy Brown, create a Compare and Contrast chart on the board. On the left side of the chart, write students' descriptions of Christy's life before he could communicate. On the right side, write their descriptions of his life after that major turning point.

Writing

Author's Craft: Sensory Language

Remind students that sensory language includes words and phrases that appeal to one or more of the five senses. Authors use sensory language to help readers "experience" and picture a scene, character, or event.

Ask students to find examples of sensory language in the selection and to explain which senses the language appeals to.

Have students sharpen their senses as they work on the writing activities on page 97.

Twenty Questions

Erma Bombeck

Selection Summary

Columnist Erma Bombeck describes a communication gap in her home. When her son arrives home late one night, she questions him about where he's been, whom he's seen, and what he's eaten. Her son, however, responds to her questions by asking questions of his own. By the time she has asked twenty questions, her son has fallen asleep.

Prereading

1. List on the board the most frequently asked questions that students face from their parents. Next to each question, write the most popular answers that students give to the questions. Then ask the following questions:
   - *What's more important, a teenager's privacy or the parents' need to know where their teenager goes and with whom?*
   - *Do you tell your parents everything you do? Why or why not?*

2. Invite a student to read the introduction on page 98 aloud. Have students predict what the selection will be about.

Active Reading

1. Students might enjoy a cooperative reading of the selection. Invite volunteers to prepare for and to read the roles of narrator; the mother; Roger, the son; and the husband. Encourage students to deliver their lines with humor.

2. Have students read the questions on page 101 silently and think about the answers.

Reading Follow-up

Discuss the questions on page 101 with the class. Bring out the following concepts:

- She wants to know where Roger has been.

- Roger responds to his mother's questions with questions that exasperate her.

- The mother is frustrated because she has asked her son twenty questions, and she still doesn't know where he's been. She is also wide awake at 1:00 in the morning.

Reading Comprehension

Recognize Author's Tone

Ask students to describe their reactions to Erma Bombeck's essay "Twenty Questions." Bombeck's humorous tone probably affected their reactions. Tone is an author's attitude toward his or her subject. The author's choice of words and details as well as descriptions of characters and events determine the tone.

Mention that although the subject of the essay—a mother's inability to communicate with her son—is an important topic, Bombeck treats it with humor. Discuss how the use of humor affects the reader's understanding of the essay.

Have students discuss other tones Bombeck might have used in writing this essay and explain how these would have affected it.

Writing

Author's Craft: Dialogue

Point out that good writers capture the subtle nuances of conversations in the dialogue they write. This makes their writing not only interesting but also more realistic. By using appropriate vocabulary and speech patterns and in some cases dialects, writers can make dialogue come alive.

Have students look through "Twenty Questions" to find examples of dialogue that sounds particularly real.

Encourage students to listen carefully to the way people speak before they begin the writing activities on page 101.

Happy Birthday

Toni Cade Bambara

Story Summary

Ollie, an orphan, spends her birthday looking for friends to play with her. Unable to find anybody to play with her, Ollie ends up in front of a local church, where even the pastor tries to send her away. Overcome with sadness because nobody acknowledges her birthday, Ollie breaks down crying.

Prereading

1. Start a concept web about birthdays on the board. Have students mention all the things they associate with birthdays.

2. Read the introduction on page 102 aloud. Have students predict why Ollie might want to shout to the world that it is her birthday.

Active Reading

1. Have students read the story silently. You can discuss the story and answer students' clarification questions after reading. Suggest that students compare Ollie to the speaker in "The Telephone."

2. Have students read the questions on page 109 silently and think about the answers.

Reading Follow-up

Discuss the questions on page 109 with the class. Bring out the following concepts:

- Ollie is an orphan who lives with her Granddaddy Larkins. On her birthday, she wanders the neighborhood looking for friends to play with her.

- "Happy Birthday" takes place on a hot summer day, which is why many people are simply relaxing and trying to stay cool.

- Ollie talks to a group of boys hanging out on a rooftop, but they tease her and tell her to leave. She talks to Reverend Hall, and he also tells her to leave. Ollie's last conversation is with Miss Hazel, who ignores the fact that it's Ollie's birthday.

Reading Comprehension

Draw Conclusions

Ask students to describe the type of person Ollie is. Point out that they have drawn conclusions about Ollie based on information in the story as well as on their own prior knowledge.

Conclusions are judgments or decisions reached after thinking about details and using common sense. Those conclusions that are supported by enough details are considered valid conclusions; those that are not are invalid conclusions.

Encourage students to continue through "Happy Birthday" and draw conclusions about the other characters.

Writing

Author's Craft: Theme

Explain to students that the theme is the central or underlying idea or message in a story. The theme reflects values or developmental learning about life itself. The theme does not teach; it helps us understand. Sometimes an author states the theme directly. But more often, a reader must figure out, or infer, what the author is trying to say.

Mention to students that stories often contain more than one theme. Have students suggest statements of theme for "Happy Birthday." They can keep the theme in mind as they work on the writing activities on page 109.

Theme Links: Communication

Using the Theme Links

Explain to the class that the activities on these pages will help them make connections between the selections they have just read and discussed and their own lives.

All students should take part in a group discussion of the theme and complete the The Theme and You activity. They may choose one of the remaining Theme Link activities or suggest another activity they would like to work on independently or with a partner or group.

Student Activities

Group Discussion
Group members may list additional questions or concepts they would like to discuss. Allow fifteen to twenty minutes for the discussions. Then have groups share their observations with the class.

Meet the Characters
Students can practice their scenes with a partner or a family member as their "audience." Encourage them to ask for feedback from the audience to help them make their scenes interesting and entertaining.

History of Communication
Students can continue this activity throughout the year by updating the museum exhibits. Encourage them to read the technology sections of newspapers and magazines to learn about new communication devices.

The Theme and You
Reassure students that everyone has problems communicating at one time or another. Encourage them to share their writing with the class, but only if they wish to do so.

Checking Theme Goals

Have students refer to the goals they noted at the beginning of this unit. Discuss their goals and outcomes with the class. Ask what they learned about the importance of communicating with others and the results of miscommunication.

Unit 4: Decisions

Building Background

Start a discussion by observing that everyone makes decisions of some kind or another, large and small, every day. Some decisions are very important and affect our lives and futures. Others are small and soon forgotten. Encourage students to share some of the decisions they make on a daily basis. Invite volunteers to talk about important decisions they have made recently. Ask them to describe the consequences of their decisions and the outcome, or what happened as a result. Use examples such as those recorded in the consequence diagram pictured below to start the discussion.

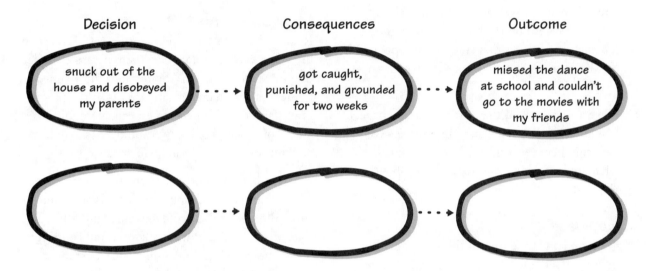

Decision   Consequences   Outcome

snuck out of the house and disobeyed my parents ----> got caught, punished, and grounded for two weeks ----> missed the dance at school and couldn't go to the movies with my friends

Previewing

Have students read and discuss the unit contents on page vii. Discuss the kinds of selections they will be reading and how they think each selection might relate to the theme. Discuss the illustration on pages 112 and 113. Ask students what kinds of decisions they think characters in the selections will make.

Reading and Discussion

Have students read the unit introduction silently and think about large and small decisions they have made. Then call on volunteers to read each paragraph aloud. Use questions like the following to guide a discussion.

- What kinds of decisions do you make every day?

- Explain the following statement: "The right to make decisions is both a privilege and a responsibility."

- Why is it sometimes hard to make decisions?

Setting Theme Goals

Help students set their own goals for reading the selections and understanding the theme. Goals might include the following:

- to read about many kinds of decisions people must make

- to understand and appreciate the consequences of decisions people make

- to learn what factors you must consider in order to make good decisions

Have students set at least two goals and write them in their notebooks. Explain that they will refer to these goals after they have read the unit selections.

Early Autumn
Langston Hughes

Story Summary

Former lovers Bill and Mary meet by chance on a cold fall afternoon in New York City. He is surprised to see how much she has aged; she longs to discuss their breakup but cannot find the words. After they part, Mary realizes that they forgot to exchange addresses and that she didn't tell Bill that she named her youngest son after him.

Prereading

1. Create a concept web about autumn. Have a volunteer record on the board the thoughts, feelings, and images that students associate with fall. Keep the web on the board as you discuss "Early Autumn."

2. Have a student read the introduction on page 114 aloud. Ask volunteers to improvise a conversation between Bill and Mary. Then discuss what students think the story will be about. Remind them to set a purpose for reading.

Active Reading

1. Give students time to read the story silently, or assign students to prepare for and read the roles of Bill, Mary, and the narrator as a readers' theater.

2. Stop at appropriate points to discuss what is happening, to clarify questions about the text, or to clear up any vocabulary problems.

3. Have students read the questions on page 117 silently and think about the answers.

Reading Follow-up

Discuss the questions on page 117 with the class. Bring out the following concepts:

- Both Bill and Mary used to live in Ohio. Each moved to New York City.

- Bill probably no longer loves Mary; he shakes her hand instead of kissing her, he frowns upon hearing that she lives in New York City, and he thinks about how old she looks.

- Mary's naming her youngest son after Bill shows that she might still have loved Bill long after her marriage.

Reading Comprehension

Story Structure: Setting/Mood

Remind students that every story is set in a certain place at a certain time. Have them describe the setting of "Early Autumn." Sometimes the setting influences the characters and events of the plot in important ways. Time is an especially important aspect of setting in "Early Autumn." Ask students to skim the story to locate references to time.

Explain that setting can also create a specific mood. Mood is the total feeling a reader gets from the story. Phrases such as cold weather, falling leaves, "late afternoon," and "nearly sunset," all contribute to the mood in "Early Autumn." Invite students to suggest words that describe the mood of the story.

Writing

Author's Craft: Dialogue

Remind students that writers use dialogue to move the story along, to reveal information, and to show the thoughts and feelings of characters. Invite volunteers to locate particularly revealing passages of dialogue in "Early Autumn" and to explain what each example reveals about the character who is speaking.

Have students keep the characters' personalities in mind as they work on the writing activities on page 117. Remind them to enclose a character's exact words in quotation marks.

Joe

Sherry Garland

Story Summary

Loi, an Amerasian girl, has just arrived in Saigon, Vietnam, where she must register at the Foreign Office before traveling to the United States. While she sleeps, a boy steals her bag, which contains a photograph of Loi's American father—the proof she'll need to get into the United States Loi catches the boy and gets her bag back, and she and the boy become friends. The boy, Joe, says that his father was an American too. Loi has good reason not to believe him, but she is impressed with his knowledge of America and of the Foreign Office. She decides to let Joe act as her brother when they go to the Foreign Office—a decision that may change her life.

Prereading

1. Ask the prereading questions below. Then start a discussion about immigration.

    • *Why do many people from countries around the world emigrate to the United States?*

    • *How have immigrants made the United States a special country?*

2. Read the introduction on page 118 aloud. Have students think of situations like this.

Active Reading

1. Call on volunteers to read the first three paragraphs aloud. Invite students to predict what they think will happen to Loi.

2. Have students read the story silently and discuss it in small groups. They can stop at appropriate points to summarize, to clarify the text, and to predict what will happen next.

3. Have students read the questions on page 131 silently and think about the answers.

Reading Follow-up

Discuss the questions on page 131 with the class. Bring out the following concepts:

• Joe meets Loi when he steals her pack. He survives by stealing and by conning people.

• Loi left home to avoid an arranged marriage. She is in Saigon to register for permission to emigrate to the United States.

• Joe's father was not American: his freckles are painted on, his hair is dyed, and his life story is filled with inaccuracies.

Reading Comprehension

Background Information

Have students locate Vietnam on a world map.

Explain that several wars have plagued Vietnam in the past fifty years. Beginning in the mid-1940s, the Vietnamese have been at war with France, the United States, Cambodia, China, and even themselves. The Vietnam War (1955-1975), in which the United States played a major role, caused widespread devastation and left millions either dead, injured, or homeless. Some American servicemen fathered children while in Vietnam and returned to the United States when their tour of duty was over, leaving their Vietnamese American children in Vietnam. This is what happened to Loi.

Writing

Author's Craft: Plot

Plot is the story line—the important events that happen in a story. A plot usually contains a central problem and a solution to that problem. When students examine the plot of a story, they should ask these questions:

• Who is the main character?
• What is his or her problem?
• What important events happen?
• How is the problem solved?

Have students think about "Joe" and then answer the questions above.

The Courtship
George Ella Lyon

Poem Summary

Soon after Sickly Jim Wilson's wife dies, he realizes that he can't maintain the farm and the house, or care for his children without the help of a wife. He lists the eligible women and sets out to talk to them. Widow Jones, the first on the list, is insulted by the proposal but nevertheless agrees to marry Jim.

Prereading

1. Ask students to tell what they know about courtships and weddings. Write their responses on the board. Then ask the following questions:
   - *Why do couples get married?*
   - *What does it take to build a successful marriage?*
   - *How has the institution of marriage changed over the years?*

2. Invite a student to read the introduction on page 132 aloud. Discuss how long students think a courtship should be.

Active Reading

1. Give students time to read the poem silently. Consider assigning the roles of narrator, Jim Wilson, and Widow Jones, and have students read the poem as readers' theater.

2. Have students read the questions on page 134 silently and think about the answers.

Reading Follow-up

Discuss the questions on page 134 with the class. Elicit the following concepts:

- Jim needs help with running the farm, keeping house, and raising his children.

- Jim makes a list of the eligible women in the area and ranks them "according to his favor."

- Widow Jones probably agrees to marry Jim because she is lonely and wants to be needed and useful.

Reading Comprehension
Make Judgments

Have students think about their answers to the prereading questions. Ask them whether reading "The Courtship" has changed their opinions. Invite volunteers to give their opinions of Sickly Jim Wilson and Widow Jones and to tell why they think as they do. Remind students that when they make judgments about characters or events in a story, they use details from the story as well as personal values, experiences, tastes, and beliefs. Making judgments about characters in a poem or story helps them connect with the literature. Point out that making judgments also involves evaluating characters and events in light of historical or cultural perspectives.

Writing
Author's Craft: News Articles

Remind students that news articles are written to inform readers. In the first paragraph of a news article, the writer will explain what the article is about, who is involved, where the event took place, when it happened, and why it happened. Point out that news articles do not contain opinions, only facts.

Have students get the facts straight as they work on the writing activities on page 134.

One Throw

W. C. Heinz

Story Summary

Eddie Brown, a New York Yankees scout, tells about the time he went to watch young Pete Maneri play in the minor leagues. To test Maneri's character, Eddie posed as a hardware salesman and suggested that Pete "throw" a game. Pete couldn't cheat. He thus won Eddie's respect and a big break into the majors.

Prereading

1. Discuss the questions below. Then ask students to talk about their favorite athletes and to explain why they admire them.
   - *What personal qualities besides talent are needed to play professional sports?*
   - *What is more important, talent or qualities such as character, determination, and heart?*

2. Invite a student to read the introduction on page 135 aloud. Have students suggest ways that the player might get a lucky break.

Active Reading

1. Give students time to read the story silently, or assign students to prepare and read the roles of Eddie Brown, the hotel desk manager, and Pete Maneri as readers' theater.

2. Have students read the questions on page 143 silently and think about the answers.

Reading Follow-up

Discuss the questions on page 143 with the class. Elicit the following concepts:

- Pete is waiting for a letter from the New York Yankees.

- Eddie pretends to be Harry Franklin so that Pete won't know that he is a scout. He wants to get to know Pete and to test his integrity.

- Eddie tells Pete to "throw" a game or two so that Dall will ask upper management to get Pete off the team. In this way, Pete will come to management's attention.

Reading Comprehension

Recognizing Foreshadowing/Making Predictions

Did students guess that Harry Franklin was really Eddie Brown? Explain that foreshadowing is a device an author uses to prepare a reader for an event or action that is to happen later in the story. Foreshadowing can be hints or bits of information revealed by the narrator that let the reader know what is to come.

Have students reread the story, looking for clues to Harry's real identity. Passages include these:
- Harry asking probing questions about Pete
- Harry saying that he recognizes Pete from pictures that he's seen
- Harry revealing that he's played baseball and has knowledge of baseball management
- Harry changing the subject when Pete asks him what he does for a living

By noticing bits of information, students can make predictions about a story.

Writing

Author's Craft: Diary Entry—Incidents

Invite students who keep diaries to explain, without getting too personal, what kinds of entries they write. Explain that diary entries usually include personal thoughts and feelings and are not intended to be read by others. Diary entries often describe incidents. They are brief retellings of events or conversations.

When writing diary entries, people usually write whatever comes into their minds, without regard to formal structure or language.

Remind students to keep their writing personal and informal as they work on the activities on page 143.

Your World

Georgia Douglas Johnson

Poem Summary

The speaker of this poem compares herself to a bird who advises readers to take chances and to pursue dreams and desires. The speaker describes how she went from living in the "narrowest nest in a corner" to making the decision to leave her nest and soar to the "uttermost reaches."

Prereading

1. Ask the prereading questions below. Then start a discussion by asking students to describe their fears and self-doubts.
   - *What are common fears that many students have?*
   - *What are the best ways to overcome a fear?*

2. Read the introduction on page 144 aloud. Discuss what people can do to change their lives. How do students think the speaker will change her life?

Active Reading

1. Let pairs of students take turns reading the poem to each other. Encourage them to use hand movements to express images and feelings as they read.

2. Have students reread the poem silently. Then have them read the questions on page 145 silently and think about the answers.

Reading Follow-up

Discuss the questions on page 145 with the class. Bring out the following concepts:

- The speaker compares herself to a bird.

- The sight of the distant horizon prompted the speaker to leave her nest.

- At the end of the poem, the speaker is free of her fears and self-doubts; she is confident, strong, and happy.

Reading Comprehension

Main Idea and Details/Stanzas

Ask students to describe how "Your World" is structured. If necessary, point out that the poem is divided into three stanzas, or groups of lines that form structural units or divisions of a poem. Clarify that in this poem the stanzas are determined by their thought or content.

Have students state the main idea of each stanza. (First stanza: The speaker describes her life before she left the nest. Second stanza: Visions of the horizon piqued the speaker's curiosity and desires. Third stanza: The speaker transcended the forces that limited her and flew.)

Writing

Poet's Craft: Rhythm and Rhyme

Invite students to repeat several popular nursery rhymes such as "Jack and Jill" and "Humpty Dumpty." Point out that these short poems are fun to read and easy to remember because they rhyme and the rhythms are infectious. Remind students that the rhythm of a poem is the pattern of stressed and unstressed syllables that repeat to give the poem its beat. The rhyme scheme is the pattern of rhyming words.

If students have difficulty with the writing activities on page 145, suggest that they write an original poem using the same rhythm and rhyme scheme as those in "Your World."

Theme Links: Decisions

Using the Theme Links

Explain to the class that the activities on these pages will help them see how reading the selections in this unit has helped them understand how the decisions they make can affect people's lives.

All students should take part in a group discussion of the theme and complete the The Theme and You activity. They may choose one of the remaining Theme Link activities or suggest another activity they would like to work on independently or with a partner or group.

Student Activities

Group Discussion

Have group members list additional questions or ideas they would like to discuss. Allow fifteen to twenty minutes for the discussions. Then have groups share their thoughts with the class.

Different Endings

You may wish to make this an ongoing class activity by having groups choose one selection from each unit, write an ending for it, and perform the new ending for the class. Post the "new" selection on a bulletin board under the heading "Different Endings."

Local (Close-to-Home) Decisions

Encourage students to carry through with their recommendations by contacting the appropriate school administrators or municipal authorities.

The Theme and You

Help students understand that every individual will make many wrong decisions in a lifetime. Point out that many people learn more from making a bad decision than from making a correct one. Encourage students to share their writing with the class.

Checking Theme Goals

Have students refer to the goals they set at the beginning of this unit. Discuss their goals and outcomes with the class. Ask what they learned about making decisions.

JAMESTOWN PUBLISHERS

Themes *in* Reading

VOLUME 2

Shirley Jackson · *Arthur Ashe* · *Jack Prelutsky*

Judith Ortiz Cofer · *Mary Helen Ponce* · *James Stevenson*

Gerald Vizenor · *Amy Tan* · *and others*

A MULTICULTURAL COLLECTION

Contents

Unit 1: Turning Points

Building Background

Discuss with the class what a turning point is. Bring out the idea that a turning point marks a change in someone's life. It could be an event that a person has no control over, something that just happens, or it could be a time of life when something happens for the first time. Moving to a new town and starting school are examples of turning points. Encourage students to share their ideas. Record the ideas in a concept web.

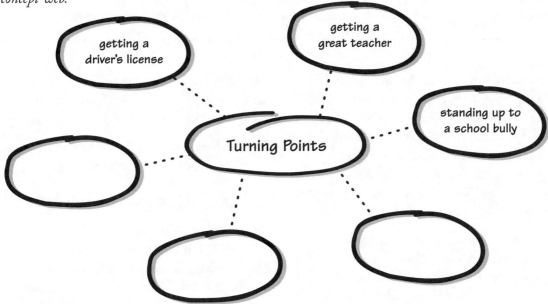

Previewing

Have students read and discuss the unit contents on page iv. Ask what kinds of selections they will be reading and how they think each selection might relate to the theme.

Then discuss the illustration on pages 2 and 3. Ask what kind of turning point each part of the illustration represents. Add any new ideas to the concept web.

Reading and Discussion

Have students read the unit introduction silently. Invite volunteers to read each paragraph aloud. Use questions like the following to guide a discussion.

• How did this introduction change your ideas of what a turning point is?

• Who would like to describe a personal turning point—a happening that affected your future? How did it change your life? What did you learn from the experience?

Setting Theme Goals

Help students set their own goals for reading the selections and understanding the theme. Goals might include the following:

• to read about different kinds of turning points

• to appreciate the important events in other people's lives

• to read interesting stories and poems

• to understand and identify turning points and how they change people's futures

Tell students to write at least two goals in their notebooks. Explain that they will refer to these goals after they have read the unit selections.

Clemente at Bat

Paul Robert Walker

Selection Summary

Seventeen-year-old Roberto Clemente's natural baseball skills impress Brooklyn Dodgers scout Al Campanis. Later, the young man is offered a professional contract—a $400 signing bonus and $40 a week to play for the Santurce Crabbers. Roberto's father believes his son is worth more money and refuses the contract. Roberto reasons with his father, who then changes his mind. As a rookie, Roberto doesn't see much action. Dejected and threatening to quit, he finally gets an opportunity to play. In the ninth inning of a game in Caguas, Roberto pinch-hits a double to win the game and the confidence of his manager.

Prereading

1. Start a flowchart that tracks the progress of an aspiring baseball player. Explain that professional players enter the big leagues by excelling at every level at which they play. Have students name as many levels of baseball as they can (little league, pony/colt/bronco league, high school, American Legion, Babe Ruth league, college, rookie league, Class A, AA, AAA, the majors).

2. Have a volunteer read the introduction on page 4 aloud. Ask students what they think the selection will be about. Have students share what they know about Roberto Clemente.

Active Reading

1. Invite volunteers to read the first six paragraphs aloud. Ask students to predict what they think will happen and why.

2. Have students read the selection silently. Stop to check and revise students' predictions.

3. Encourage students to compare and contrast young Roberto Clemente and Pete Maneri in the story "One Throw." Then have them read the questions on page 15 silently and think about the answers.

Reading Follow-up

Discuss the questions on page 15 with the class. Bring out the following concepts:

• Roberto and the other players are excited about the tryouts because the color barrier in major league baseball had recently been broken. They believe that good players from Puerto Rico could play in the big leagues.

• Roberto's father thinks that Pedrín Zorilla is underpaying Roberto. Zorilla and Roberto think $400 is fair because Roberto is inexperienced.

• Zorilla doesn't like to play rookies so they won't get discouraged if they aren't successful.

Reading Comprehension

Background Information

Born in 1934 in Puerto Rico, Roberto Clemente began his major league career in 1955 with the Pittsburgh Pirates. Clemente won many awards, and he led the Pirates to the 1960 World Series championship. Clemente was also known for his off-field humanitarian efforts. He died in a plane crash in 1972 while taking relief supplies to earthquake survivors in Nicaragua. In 1973, Roberto was inducted into the Baseball Hall of Fall.

Writing

Author's Craft: Biography

A biography, a true account of a real person's life written by another person, may not tell about a person's whole life; it may describe only part of it. Also, a biography contains only facts about the person's life, although an author may invent realistic dialogue or small details to add interest. The biographer may express an opinion about the subject of the biography by telling why the person is important.

Fifteen

William Stafford

Poem Summary

Near a road, the speaker finds a motorcycle lying on its side with its engine running. The motorcycle presents him with a dilemma. Should he give in to the impulse to drive away, or should he look for the owner? The poem captures the inner conflict of a fifteen-year-old torn between freedom and responsibility.

Prereading

1. Start a concept web about being fifteen years old. Ask students to describe the thoughts and feelings that they associate with being fifteen. Then start a discussion about people who recall their teen years as happy and carefree. Point out that for many people, though, the teenage years are also a time of conflict. Describe a time during your teens when you felt torn between freedom and responsibility.

2. Invite a student to read the introduction on page 16 aloud. Encourage students to discuss what they think the poem will be about.

Active Reading

1. Have students read the poem silently. Then ask volunteers to read the poem aloud, emphasizing the emotions and feelings evident in it.

2. Have students read the questions on page 18 silently and think about the answers.

Reading Follow-up

Discuss the questions on page 18 with the class. Elicit the following concepts:

- The driver of the motorcycle had an accident. He lost control of the vehicle, flipped over the guardrail, and was knocked unconscious.

- The speaker wants to drive away on the motorcycle. He imagines what it would be like to "find the end of a road" or "meet / the sky out on Seventeenth."

- The speaker changes his mind after he imagines himself riding away on the motorcycle. At that point, he begins to think about the driver. The speaker's decision to look for the owner is a move toward adulthood. Instead of giving in to the impulse to drive away, the speaker acts responsibly.

Reading Comprehension

Vocabulary: Connotation and Denotation

Point out that "Fifteen" is filled with language rich in connotative meaning. Explain that most words have both denotations (dictionary definitions) and connotations (ideas or emotions associated with denotations). To illustrate the difference between the two types of meanings, have students discuss the denotations and connotations of the words *cheap* and *inexpensive*.

Ask students to identify and discuss the denotations and connotations of some of the words in "Fifteen." Include descriptions such as "pulsing gleam," "shiny flanks," and "demure headlights."

Writing

Author's Craft: Personification

Remind students that personification is a figure of speech in which an idea or nonhuman thing is given human attributes or feelings. Ask students to find examples of personification in the poem.

Point out that personification allows a poet to describe with energy and vitality an object or idea that might otherwise have remained inanimate and uninteresting.

Tell students to keep these points in mind as they work on the writing activities on page 18.

On With My Life
Patti Trull

Selection Summary

Just before her sixteenth birthday, Patti Trull is diagnosed with cancer. To halt the spread of the disease, the doctors plan to amputate her leg. To make matters worse, test results show that a tumor has formed in one of her lungs as well. The doctors soon offer Patti a new type of chemotherapy drug for ten weeks before reexamining the need to amputate her leg. In those ten weeks, Patti focuses on enjoying life and not dwelling on her illness. In the process she comes to accept the illness and resigns herself to battling it.

Prereading

1. Ask the prereading questions below. Then start a discussion about serious illnesses.
   * *Have you or anyone you know been diagnosed with a serious illness?*
   * *What thoughts and feelings did you have when you received the news of the illness?*

2. Ask a student to read the introduction on page 19 aloud. Discuss what students think the selection will be about, and help them set a purpose for reading.

Active Reading

1. Invite volunteers to read the first two paragraphs aloud. Ask students to predict what they think will happen and why. Write their predictions on the chalkboard.

2. Have students read the selection silently. Suggest that they keep a list of medical terms they find in the selection.

3. Have students read the questions on page 29 silently and think about the answers.

Reading Follow-up

Discuss the questions on page 29 with the class. Bring out the following concepts:

* The emotions Patti feels on the morning of the hospital visit include fear, denial, anger, resentment, betrayal, anxiety, and disbelief. They were all brought on by the hospital tests and the news that she has cancer.

* Patti doesn't believe the doctor when he tells her that she has cancer.

* Patti finally accepts her illness by focusing on the good things in her life and by realizing that life goes on no matter what happens. As she says, "You either go with it or you stop living."

Reading Comprehension

Specialized Vocabulary

Ask students to identify the medical terms used in the story as you list them on the board. Discuss the meanings. Ask students what clues they used to try to figure out the meanings. Point out that when writing about particular fields, occupations, or subjects, such as medicine, authors use specialized vocabularies to describe technical aspects of the topics. Mention to students that thinking about how a group of words relate to one another can help them learn the words' meanings.

Encourage students to continue listing specialized vocabulary for this selection and for those to come.

Writing

Author's Craft: Autobiography

Remind students that an autobiography is the story of someone's life written by that person. Since an autobiography is written in the first person, it can include many examples of how the subject felt and what the subject said.

Discuss the differences between an autobiography and a biography. Then have students work on the writing activities on page 29.

The White Umbrella

Gish Jen

Story Summary

A Chinese American narrator recalls an incident when she was twelve years old and trying to act more "American." While at her piano lesson, she sees a beautiful white umbrella and wrongly assumes that it belongs to Eugenie, who is attractive and popular at school, and is also a good pianist. The umbrella symbolizes American culture to the narrator. The piano instructor then gives the narrator the umbrella, which is actually hers, as a gift. The narrator tells the instructor that she wishes she were her mother. On the way home with her mother and sister after the lesson, their car is involved in an accident, and the narrator thinks her mother has been seriously injured. The narrator recalls what she said to her piano instructor. Feeling guilty, the narrator throws the white umbrella down a sewer drain.

Prereading

1. Ask the prereading questions below. Let students discuss what it means to be "American."
   - *Have you ever felt different from everyone around you? How did it make you feel?*
   - *How did you overcome your feelings of isolation?*

2. Read the introduction on page 30 aloud. Discuss what students think the story will be about and help them set a purpose for reading.

Active Reading

1. Invite volunteers to read the first two paragraphs aloud. Encourage students to predict what they think will happen. Write their predictions on the chalkboard.

2. Give students time to read the story silently.

3. Have students read the questions on page 43 silently and think about the answers.

Reading Follow-up

Discuss the questions on page 43 with the class. Bring out the following concepts:

- The white umbrella represents American culture—the culture that the narrator wishes to be a part of.

- The narrator admires Eugenie because she is popular and attractive, is a good pianist, and owns a lovely umbrella.

- The girls are afraid to tell anyone that their mother works because they are embarrassed that she has to help support the family.

Reading Comprehension

Recognize Conflict

Describe the two major kinds of conflict in literature—external and internal. An external conflict is a physical or verbal struggle between characters or a physical struggle between a character and nature. An internal conflict involves conscience or conflicting emotions. External conflicts often cause internal conflicts.

Point out that identifying the conflict in a story will help students focus on how characters' change and help them understand the theme better. Ask students to describe the conflict in "The White Umbrella." (The narrator's conflict is internal.)

Writing

Author's Craft: Descriptive Writing

Explain that most good writers are keen observers. When they write about characters or a scene, they use descriptive details that accurately and interestingly portray that subject. Vivid descriptions are created by using specific nouns, action verbs, and interesting and precise adjectives. Ask students to find examples of descriptive language in "The White Umbrella."

Students should keep these points in mind as they work on the writing activities on page 43.

Freedom

Charlotte Painter

Selection Summary

In this short sketch, the writer describes Alice Lindberg Snyder's trip to a shoe store to buy tap shoes. In relating the incident, the writer reveals bits and pieces of Alice's life. Alice is in her seventies, and her husband has died recently. To cope with the grief, she has decided to make the most of every day and to allow her fun-loving nature to resurface. This selection illustrates how a tragic event like the death of a spouse can become a turning point for the survivor.

Prereading

1. Have students fill in a Venn diagram on the board to compare and contrast the lifestyles of young people and elderly people. Invite volunteers to share their opinions on why these differences exist. Encourage students to describe people they know who don't act their age.

2. Invite a volunteer to read the introduction on page 44 aloud. Discuss what students think the selection will be about, and help them set a purpose for reading.

Active Reading

1. Give students time to read the selection silently. Encourage them to work with a partner to clarify any questions they have about the text.

2. Have students read the questions on page 47 silently and think about the answers.

Reading Follow-up

Discuss the questions on page 47 with the class. Bring out the following concepts:

• At first the shoe salesman is surprised that Alice wants tap shoes. But he fits her anyway and then encourages her to do a demonstration.

• Alice's husband has died. To cope with the loss, she went to a therapist who convinced her to live each day to the fullest.

• Alice accepts the fact that she is in the later years of her life. She wants to become all she can be in her remaining years by letting the fun-loving nature of childhood take over. Buying tap shoes, thinking of rafting with her grandson, and abandoning her previous lifestyle are details that illustrate her new-found zest for life.

Reading Comprehension

Recognize Stereotypes

Explain that a stereotype is a simplified conception or image of a person or group of people. Have students describe some common stereotypes. Encourage them to discuss where these stereotypes originate.

Ask students whether they were surprised that an elderly woman like Alice would be buying tap shoes. Have students look through the selection for other examples of stereotyping.

Writing

Author's Craft: Tone

Remind students that tone is the author's attitude toward the subject or audience. The author's choice of words and details, as well as descriptions of characters and events, determine the tone. Point out that the author's tone often affects the way readers react to an essay or selection.

Ask students to identify the tone of the essay. Possible answers include supportive, positive, and praising. Encourage students to explain how they determined the tone. Invite students to discuss or rewrite portions of the selection using other tones. Have students discuss how a different tone might change their overall reaction to the selection.

Have students keep these points in mind as they work on the writing activities on page 47.

Theme Links: Turning Points

Using the Theme Links

The activities on these pages will help students make connections between the selections they have just read and discussed and their own lives.

All students should participate in a group discussion of the theme and complete the The Theme and You activity. Students may choose to work on one of the remaining Theme Link activities, or they may suggest another activity they would like to work on independently or with a partner or group.

Student Activities

Group Discussion

Encourage participants to list additional questions or concepts they would like to discuss. Allow fifteen to twenty minutes for the discussions. Then have groups share their observations with the class.

The Characters: Monologue

Students can practice their monologues at home. Suggest that they ask their parents or family members to be the audience. Encourage students to ask for feedback from the audience to help them make their monologues accurate and interesting.

The Characters: Patti and Alice

Have students work with a partner to create and practice the role-play. Then invite volunteers to perform their role-play for the class.

Your Choice

If your class has created a "Different Endings" bulletin board for new endings (see TG page 31, "Different Endings"), you may wish to videotape or photograph a few scenes of one or several of the role-plays and add them to the display.

The Theme and You

Help students understand that each of them will experience turning points in their lives. Encourage those who wish to do so to share their writing with the class.

Checking Theme Goals

Have students refer to the goals they set at the beginning of this unit. Discuss their goals and outcomes with the class. Ask what they might add to the concept web they worked on before reading the unit.

Unit 2: Families

Building Background

Discuss with the class what a family is. Encourage students to describe their families. Invite them to talk about how family members should treat each other and how to keep family relationships strong. Record their ideas on a family tree.

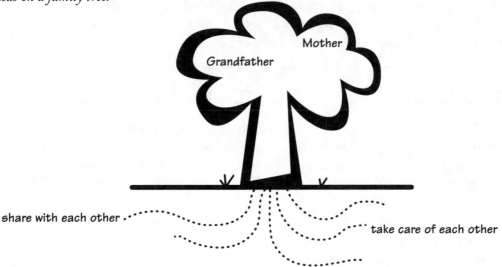

Previewing

Have students read and discuss the unit contents on page v. Encourage students to talk about what kinds of selections they will be reading and how they think each selection might relate to the theme.

Discuss the illustration on pages 50 and 51. Ask students to describe the people in the illustration and to explain what kinds of families or relationships the illustration reveals. Add any new ideas to the family tree.

Reading and Discussion

Have students read the unit introduction silently and think about the answers to the questions it asks.

Invite volunteers to read each paragraph aloud. After each paragraph, stop to discuss students' answers to the questions. Make a list of various family members and relationships on the chalkboard as students volunteer them.

Have students share their families' cultural customs and beliefs with the class.

Use questions like the following to help guide the discussion.

- How did this introduction make you think about your family relationships?

- Who would like to talk about their family? What makes your family special? What do you like best about your family?

- What family member do you have a special relationship with?

Setting Theme Goals

Help students set their own goals for reading the selections and understanding the theme. Goals might include the following:

- to read about different kinds of families

- to appreciate a variety of family relationships

- to read interesting stories and poems

- to understand the role families play in people's lives

Tell students to set at least two goals and write them in their notebooks. Explain that they will refer to these goals after they have read the unit selections.

A New Arrival

S h i r l e y   J a c k s o n

Selection Summary

Author Shirley Jackson and her husband arrive home from the hospital with their newborn son. Jackson humorously relates how her three older children react to their new baby brother—someone they are not sure will be an asset to the family.

Prereading

1. Invite students to share humorous stories they've heard or experienced about children's reactions to a new baby. Rank the stories according to how funny they are.

2. Have students preview the story and notice the quotation marks. Point out that these signal that much of the story is told in dialogue.

Active Reading

1. You may wish to have students read the selection silently and discuss it in small groups. Suggest that they stop at appropriate points to summarize or to discuss a clarification question.

2. After students have read the story silently, they may read it in a group with one student acting as narrator and others reading the dialogue of the various family members.

3. Have students read the questions on page 56 silently and think about the answers.

Reading Follow-up

Discuss the questions on page 56 with the class. Bring out the following concepts:

• Jackson and her husband are returning from the hospital. They are bringing home their newborn baby.

• Sally is too young to understand where the baby came from; Jannie and Laurie think the baby is too small; Laurie is quickly bored by the event.

• Laurie thinks the baby will be a good addition to the family because it will give his mother something to do, now that (he thinks) he and his sisters are all grown up.

Reading Comprehension

Recognize Author's Tone

Ask students what made the children's reactions to the new baby humorous. What makes the whole selection humorous? Point out that Jackson's tone affects the way readers react to the selection. Remind students that tone is an author's attitude toward his or her subject. The author's choice of words and details, as well as descriptions of characters and events, determine the tone.

Invite students to discuss and even rewrite portions of the selection using another tone. Have students share their writing and discuss how a different tone changes their overall reaction to the selection.

Writing

Author's Craft: Journal Entries

Remind students that a journal records specific experiences of a person's life. Journal entries are usually very descriptive and often relate memorable incidents, special events, important conversations, or other happenings. Like diaries, journals contain personal opinions, beliefs, and feelings. Unlike diaries, however, journals are often kept as historical records by people, eventually to be made public.

Have students complete the writing activities on page 56.

An Hour With Abuelo

Judith Ortiz Cofer

Story Summary

Arturo's mother asks him to visit his elderly abuelo (grandfather) at the nursing home. Despite arguing that he's too busy and that he doesn't like going to the home, Arturo goes. In his abuelo's suite, Arturo listens as the old man tells his life story. In relating his story, Abuelo sheds light on a man Arturo never knew. Arturo comes to respect and admire him.

Prereading

1. Ask the prereading questions below. Then start a discussion about grandparents and other relatives.
   - *Is it important to be close to your grandparents?*
   - *What can you learn from grandparents?*

2. Have students skim the story to find Spanish words and phrases. List them on the board and let volunteers translate them into English.

Active Reading

1. Invite volunteers to read the first two paragraphs aloud. Ask students to predict whether Arturo will visit his abuelo and what his visit will be like. List the predictions on the board.

2. Let students read the story silently; then have them prepare and present an oral reading. Encourage students to read Arturo's lines in the breezy, informal style that characterizes his speech. Tell students that they should examine the feelings underlying what he says about himself and his abuelo. Ask whether what Arturo says completely explains his behavior and his attitude.

3. Have students read the questions on page 64 silently and think about the answers.

Reading Follow-up

Discuss the questions on page 64 with the class. Elicit the following concepts:

- Arturo avoids visiting his abuelo because summer vacation is almost over, he has books to read, and he doesn't like the "old people's home."

- Arturo's basically a good boy but perhaps a bit self-centered. Arturo's abuelo is reflective and regrets that he never returned to teaching. He is still alert and sharp.

- Arturo's abuelo is proud of his family and of teaching them to read and write. He also wanted to remain a teacher rather than be a farmer.

Reading Comprehension

Summarize

Arturo and his abuelo relate a lot of background information in "An Hour With Abuelo." Remind students that summarizing important information will help them keep track of story events and better understand what happens.

Invite volunteers to summarize the following:
- Arturo's thoughts and feelings about his abuelo
- Arturo's abuelo's life
- How Arturo's attitude changes after spending an hour with his abuelo

Writing

Author's Craft: Formal and Informal Language

Point out that "An Hour With Abuelo" is written in an informal style. Informal English is used in most magazines, newspapers, and writing intended for general audiences. Some writers include slang and try to capture the ways in which people actually talk.

Tell students that formal language is used for serious writing, such as essays, reports, research papers, literary criticism, and scholarly works. Formal English uses long, elaborately constructed sentences. Contractions and slang are rare.

Encourage students to skim through the selection to identify passages that contain informal language. Then have them work on the writing activities on page 64.

Small Song for Daddy
W. D. Ehrhart

Poem Summary

The speaker of the poem is awakened by his infant daughter at 1:00 A.M. As he holds her, he marvels at the sound of her small voice and at the sense of wonder with which she regards everyday objects around her. He reflects that she is completely unaware that her wordless song fills a need within him.

Prereading

1. Start a concept web about babies. Ask students to contribute words and descriptions they associate with babies.

2. Invite a student to read the introduction on page 65 aloud. Then have students discuss their experiences with babies.

Active Reading

1. Have students read the poem silently. Then ask volunteers to take turns reading the poem aloud, emphasizing the father's emotions.

2. Have students read the questions on page 67 silently and think about the answers.

Reading Follow-up

Discuss the questions on page 67 with the class. Elicit the following concepts:

• The daughter is an infant. She has some control over her arms and legs and looks closely at objects, but she doesn't know how to talk yet.

• The daughter is contented. She plays with the hair on her father's chest, wiggles her toes, and sings softly.

• At first the father is concerned because his daughter usually doesn't wake up at that hour of the night. He then feels relieved that she is all right. The father takes pleasure in watching and listening to the baby. He also feels a sense of fulfillment from listening to her song.

Reading Comprehension

Personal Experience

Have students review the concept web they started at the beginning of this lesson. Mention to students that one way to better understand and appreciate the poem is by recalling their own experiences with babies. Suggest that students ask the following questions:

• How are my experiences with babies similar to or different from the speaker's?

• Based on my experiences, do the speaker's feelings and ideas about babies seem realistic?

• What do my experiences add to my understanding of the poem?

Ask students to read the poem again, encouraging them to point out passages that describe familiar feelings or situations.

Writing

Author's Craft: Similes

Remind students that a simile is a direct comparison in which one thing is said to be like something else. A simile uses the word *like* or *as*.

Invite students to make up similes for the following situations. Encourage students to come up with several ideas for each.

• As he sat in the dentist's waiting room, his heart pounded like _____

• The sunset looked like _____

• The July afternoon was as hot as _____

Ask students to find the similes in the poem. Then have them complete the writing activities on page 67.

Nicknames

Gerald Vizenor

Story Summary

A young Chippewa Indian narrator tells about her great-uncle Clement, whom everyone calls Almost. Almost is responsible for giving nicknames to all the members of the narrator's family. The narrator describes how she received her nickname and what it means.

Prereading

Ask the prereading questions below.

- *What is your nickname? Explain how it was that you received the name.*
- *What do you think of your nickname? Does it make a difference who calls you by the nickname? Explain.*

Active Reading

1. Invite volunteers to read the first two paragraphs aloud. Encourage students to talk about Almost and the narrator. Have volunteers predict what they think Almost will do or say and write their predictions on the chalkboard.

2. Because this selection has an oral storytelling feel to it, have students prepare to read a section of text and take turns reading aloud. Stop at appropriate points to discuss what they've read or whenever someone has a clarification question.

3. Have students read the questions on page 72 silently and think about the answers.

Reading Follow-up

Discuss the questions on page 72 with the class. Elicit the following concepts:

- The narrator likes and admires Almost. She listens intently to his stories, and she has obviously spent a great deal of time with him.

- Almost gave her the nickname Pincher because she learned about the world between two fingers. She pinched everything—animals, insects, leaves, water, fish, ice cream, air, winter breath, snow, and even words.

- When the grandmother died, the narrator's family calmly accepted her death and were comforted because they believed she pinched a warm summer word before she died.

Reading Comprehension

Understanding Character Motivation

Point out that it is important for readers to think about character motivation—the reasons that characters do what they do and say what they say. Have students think of questions they would like to ask Almost to help them understand why he acts as he does. Use the following questions as examples:

- Why do you feel it's important to give nicknames to everyone in your family?
- Why is *almost* your favorite word?

Write students' responses on the board. Encourage them to continue through the story, identifying passages or asking questions that might help explain why a character acts as he or she does.

Writing

Author's Craft: Descriptive Language

Remind students that good writers are good observers. When describing a character or a scene, good writers use vivid details to accurately and interestingly portray their subjects. Invite a volunteer to tell several ways that writers create vivid descriptions (by using specific nouns, action verbs, and interesting and precise adjectives).

Ask students to find examples of descriptive language in the selection.

Remind students to use vivid details as they work on the writing activities on page 72.

My Reputation

Arthur Ashe

Selection Summary

In this excerpt from his autobiography, Arthur Ashe explains that his reputation is his most prized possession. Ashe tells several anecdotes about experiences in his life that shaped his character. In the process, he talks about his deep love and admiration for his father and the lessons that he learned from him.

Prereading

1. Ask these prereading questions. List the various reputations people might have.
   - *How does a person develop a reputation?*
   - *What reputation are you trying to build? Why?*

2. Have students skim the selection to identify difficult words to look up before they read. Let them find the meanings of those words and share them in class.

Active Reading

1. Arthur Ashe was born in 1943 in Richmond, Virginia. He was the first African American tennis player to win a major men's singles championship. He won the 1975 Wimbledon singles and World Championship singles, and he ranked first in world tennis. He criticized the South African racial policy of apartheid, which led to South Africa's being excluded from Davis Cup competition. In 1993, Ashe revealed that he had contracted the AIDS virus from a blood transfusion. He died in 1993.

2. Let students read the selection silently. Ask volunteers to read aloud passages that describe the relationships between Arthur Ashe and his father and other family members.

3. Have students read the questions on page 79 silently and think about the answers.

Reading Follow-up

Discuss the questions on page 79 with the class. Bring out the following concepts:

- Ashe loves and respects his father—a strong, dutiful, and providing man, as well as the most influential person in Arthur's life.

- The most important lesson Arthur Senior taught his son was about reputation: "What people think of you, . . . is all that counts."

- Arthur and his father had a strong and very trusting relationship. Arthur's word and reputation were solid with his father.

Reading Comprehension

Fact and Opinion

Remind students that a fact is a statement that can be proved correct. An opinion expresses a person's judgments, feelings, or beliefs, none of which can be proved or verified.

Point out to students that distinguishing between fact and opinion will help them evaluate the accuracy of what they read. It will also help them identify an author's attitudes, beliefs, or feelings about an issue.

Ask students to reread "My Reputation" and identify facts and opinions. Suggest that when students read a statement, they ask, "Can this statement be proved?" If it can, the statement is probably a fact; if it can't, it is probably an opinion.

Writing

Author's Craft: Anecdotes and Incidents

An anecdote is a story within a story that illustrates a point or tells what a character or person is like. Arthur Ashe uses anecdotes to describe his father and to illustrate how important his reputation is. Have students locate and read aloud these anecdotes. Invite a volunteer to explain the point of each one.

Then allow time for students to work on the writing activities on page 79.

Theme Links: Families

Using the Theme Links

The activities on these pages will help students make connections between the selections they have just read and discussed and their own lives.

All students should take part in a group discussion of the theme and complete the The Theme and You activity. Let students choose one of the remaining Theme Link activities or suggest another activity they would like to work on independently or with a partner or group.

Student Activities

Group Discussion
Encourage group members to list additional questions or concepts they would like to discuss. Allow fifteen to twenty minutes for the discussions. Then have groups share their observations with the class.

Hearing from the Characters
Suggest that students audiotape their speeches and listen to the tape to help them revise. They can also ask a partner to give feedback and suggestions for making their speech more interesting.

Talking About Babies
Encourage students to review "Small Song for Daddy" and "A New Arrival" to make their conversations authentic and consistent with the characters' ages and way of speaking.

Your Family
You may wish to turn this activity into a class project by making a class scrapbook with a page or spread for each student. You might "feature" one student each day by having the student discuss his or her part of the scrapbook.

The Theme and You
Invite volunteers to read their poems aloud to the class. Encourage observations from the class about what makes each poem or family interesting and unique.

Checking Theme Goals

Have students refer to the goals they set at the beginning of this unit. Discuss their goals and outcomes with the class. Ask what they have learned about families and relationships and what they might now add to the family tree they worked on before reading the unit.

Unit 3: Memories

Building Background

Start a class discussion by asking students what they think a unit titled Memories will be about. Ask what kinds of things they remember. Discuss the different types of memories people have. Encourage students to talk about their own memories. Record their ideas and responses in a chart like the one below.

Memories

Happy	Sad	News		
– when my sister was born – last day of school	– day we moved – the time my pet died			

Previewing

Have students read and discuss the unit contents on page vi. Discuss the kinds of selections they will be reading and ask how they think each selection might relate to the theme.

Then discuss the illustration on pages 82 and 83. Ask students what kind of memory they think each part of the illustration might represent. Add any new ideas about memories to the chart.

Reading and Discussion

Have students read the unit introduction silently and think about the answers to the questions. Then call on volunteers to read each paragraph aloud. Questions like the following will help guide a discussion.

- What memories did you think about after reading this introduction?

- Who would like to share a vivid memory? What makes the memory special? How does it make you feel?

Setting Theme Goals

Help students set their own goals for reading the selections and understanding the theme. Goals might include the following:

- to read about different kinds of memories

- to appreciate and learn from the memories of others

- to read interesting stories and poems

- to understand why memories are important and learn to cherish them

Tell students to write at least two goals in their notebooks. Remind them that they will return to these goals after they have read the unit selections.

Concha

M a r y   H e l e n   P o n c e

Story Summary

A narrator recalls the games she and her friends played while growing up in a barrio in California. The most memorable games involved the treacherous red ants that invaded the area every summer. Concha, the narrator's best friend, was the bravest of all. She never lost her nerve, even when the ants crawled up her leg or when ornery wasps landed in her hair.

Prereading

1. Invite students to describe the games they played when they were younger. Then ask the following prereading questions:
   - *Why do many kids enjoy playing with insects?*
   - *What is the most memorable incident involving an insect that you can recall?*

2. Explain that the story contains many Spanish words and phrases, usually preceded or followed by their English translation. Tell students to list these Spanish expressions as they read.

Active Reading

1. Invite volunteers to read the first two paragraphs aloud. Ask what the Spanish phrases *para divertirnos* and *los pirules* mean in English. Have students describe the narrator and tell whether they know anyone like her.

2. Have students choose partners and read the story silently. Encourage them to stop and clarify the meanings of Spanish expressions, to discuss what they've read, or to answer questions.

3. Ask students to read the questions on page 90 silently and to think about the answers.

Reading Follow-up

Discuss the questions on page 90 with the class. Bring out the following concepts:

- The narrator and her friends played with pea shooters and whistles made from long blades of grass. They also played the game "kick the can" and made up various games with ants.

- The narrator and her friends were regular kids. They played the same kinds of games kids play everywhere.

- Most of the kids admired Concha's bravery when it came to insects, except Mundo, who thought that Concha was a big show-off.

Reading Comprehension

Personal Experiences

Remind students that recalling their own experiences is one way to understand and appreciate a story or characters. Let students ask themselves the following questions as they discuss "Concha":

- How are my experiences similar to or different from the narrator's?

- Based on my experiences, do the narrator's stories and descriptions seem reasonable?

- How do my experiences help me understand Concha, the narrator, or the whole story?

Writing

Author's Craft: Dialogue

Invite volunteers to describe the uses of dialogue. Students should know that writers use dialogue to
- move the story along
- reveal information
- show the thoughts and feelings of characters

Good writers try to capture the way people actually talk. Have students work in small groups to locate interesting passages of dialogue in the story. Then have them brainstorm words and phrases that these people might use to describe
- an action movie
- a five-year-old girl
- a college mathematics professor
- a rock-and-roll star

Have students complete the activities on page 90.

Everette Tharp's Memories of Appalachia

Guy and Candie Carawan

Selection Summary

In this essay, an elderly man—Everette Tharp—describes his memories of growing up and living in Appalachia in the early twentieth century, when people depended on the land for survival.

Prereading

1. On a United States map, point out the mountains of eastern Kentucky. Ask students what it might have been like to live in that area 100 years ago. Brainstorm a list of terms to describe life in that region at that time.

2. Read the introduction on page 91 aloud. Have students outline Appalachia on a United States map. Invite students to find information about Appalachia to share with the class.

Active Reading

1. Invite volunteers to read the first two paragraphs aloud and then describe Tharp's farm.

2. Have students read the story silently. Stop at appropriate points to discuss what they've read or to answer questions.

3. Have students read the questions on page 93 silently and think about the answers.

Reading Follow-up

Discuss the questions on page 93 with the class. Bring out the following concepts:

• Life in Appalachia in the early 1900s was much simpler than it is today. People enjoyed nature, but their lives were hard.

• The railroad changed Appalachia.

• Tharp misses the "mountain man" way of life, and the time when people respected honor and truth.

Have students compare their prereading lists with descriptions in the selection. Discuss the differences.

Reading Comprehension

Main Idea and Details

Can students state the main idea of "Memories of Appalachia"? Remind them that the main idea tells what a whole selection, chapter, or paragraph is about. Each main idea is supported by details. Sometimes the main idea is stated in one sentence (explicit). Writers often state the main idea in the opening sentence of a paragraph. Other times the main idea is unstated (implicit): readers must infer the main idea from details.

Have students examine each paragraph in the selection to identify the main idea and tell whether it's explicit or implicit. (Paragraph 1: implicit—Tharp's life was rustic; paragraph 2: implicit—Tharp knew nature and animals; paragraph 3: explicit—sentence 1 states main idea; paragraph 4: explicit—in Tharp's time, people were honorable; paragraph 5: explicit— railroads unraveled Tharp's way of life.)

Writing

Author's Craft: Details

Remind students that main ideas are supported by details. Details can include facts and statistics, incidents, examples, quotations, opinions, or visual aids. Each detail should relate to the main idea.

Have students list the details that support the main idea of each paragraph and tell whether the main idea is explicit or implicit.

Remind students to keep these points in mind as they work on the writing activities on page 93.

Seeing Snow
Gustavo Pérez - Firmat

Poem Summary

A speaker describes the confusion and isolation he feels whenever he sees snow. The speaker was born in a country where it has never snowed, so he considers seeing snow a "suspension of the laws of nature." The speaker also questions why he is "here" and whether he has lost his way.

Prereading

1. Start a concept web about snow by asking students to describe the thoughts and feelings they associate with it. Discuss their most memorable experiences with snow or what they think living in a place where it snows would be like.

2. Invite a student to read the introduction on page 94 aloud. Discuss with the class why seeing snow might make a person feel out of place.

Active Reading

1. Have students read the poem silently. Then ask volunteers to take turns reading the poem aloud, emphasizing the emotions and feelings of confusion the speaker has.

2. Have students read the questions on page 96 silently and think about the answers.

Reading Follow-up

Discuss the questions on page 96 with the class. Elicit the following concepts:

• The speaker was born and raised in another country where it never snows; he still isn't used to seeing snow in his new homeland.

• The speaker is probably from a country south of the United States. His father and grandfather speak another language.

• The speaker is surprised that he lives where it snows. He also feels out of place or lost, asking, "What, exactly, am I doing here? / Whose house is this anyway?" He ends the poem on a mysterious or positive note, however, by using the word *yet*.

Reading Comprehension

Generate Questions

Ask students to describe parts of the poem that are confusing or interesting or that leave them wanting to know more. One way to gain a better understanding and appreciation of a poem is by asking questions about it. Just as the speaker asks questions— "What, exactly, am I doing here?/Whose house is this anyway?"—readers can ask questions, too.

Help students generate questions by sharing your own questions about the poem.
• Where do the speaker's father and grandfather live?
• Why did the speaker leave his homeland?
• Where does the speaker live now?
• Will the speaker ever go back to his homeland?

Invite students to share and discuss their questions about "Seeing Snow."

Writing

Poet's Craft: Theme

Remind students that theme is the underlying idea or message in a poem. Explain that usually the theme of a poem does not teach; it helps us understand life and often raises more questions. To help students examine the theme, suggest that they first identify the major conflict that the main character or speaker is grappling with.

Have volunteers describe the theme in "Seeing Snow." Possible answers include dealing with isolation from one's family or questioning one's existence or purpose in life. Point out that in poetry the theme usually is not stated directly. A reader must figure out what the author is trying to say.

Ask students to consider these points as they work on the writing activities on page 96.

Day of the Refugios

Alberto Ríos

Poem Summary

A speaker named Refugio tells how she follows in a long line of women named Refugio in her family. She recalls her childhood in Arizona, when her family celebrated día de los Refugios *(the day of the Refugios)—the saint's day of people named Refugio—rather than the Fourth of July. She describes the tradition of that special day and the pride she takes in her Mexican heritage.*

Prereading

1. Ask the prereading questions below. Then start a discussion about students' names.
   - *What makes a good name?*
   - *Some cultures allow individuals to pick their own names. Do you think that is a good idea? Why or why not?*

2. Read the introduction on page 97 aloud. Suggest that students think about how this family's Fourth of July compares with the way they themselves celebrate the holiday.

Active Reading

1. Give students time to read the poem silently. Then read it again in a cooperative reading. Organize students into groups of three. Have each group member read one line from each three-line stanza.

2. Have students read the questions on page 100 silently and think about the answers.

Reading Follow-up

Discuss the questions on page 100 with the class. Bring out the following concepts:

- The speaker thinks Refugio is a good name because it is a "real" name, a colorful name that is serious and that takes a moment to pronounce.

- The speaker respects and takes pride in her heritage. She is proud of the tradition of her name in her family and the strong connection to the saints.

- The Day of the Refugios is important to the speaker because it is a reminder of her Mexican heritage and of Mexico, which her family left.

Reading Comprehension

Summarizing

Ask a volunteer to summarize "Day of the Refugios." Remind students that a summary is a short way of telling what a story or poem is about. It includes the most important information—the characters, setting, events, and problems—and helps readers keep track of what happens or what's described. Point out that it is easier to summarize parts of a piece of literature than to summarize the whole piece.

Have students summarize the main idea of each stanza so that they can see the logic or purpose underlying the stanza breaks.

Writing

Author's Craft: Mood

Explain to students that mood is the feeling that a work of literature conveys to a reader. The feeling may be peaceful, mysterious, joyful, haunting, and so on. The mood of a poem is created through an author's choice of words, particularly descriptive details.

Invite students to describe the mood of "Day of the Refugios." (Possible answers include the following: joyful, serious, celebratory.)

Have students complete the writing activities on page 100.

Two Kinds

Amy Tan

Story Summary

In this chapter from The Joy Luck Club, *Jing-mei Woo recounts her mother's attempts to make her into a child prodigy. Mrs. Woo arranges for Jing-mei to take piano lessons, but the girl makes no attempt to practice or to learn. When Jing-mei performs in a talent show, she plays terribly. After the show, Mrs. Woo tries to force Jing-mei to resume her music lessons. In the ensuing argument, the angry daughter says something that breaks her mother's determination forever. Years later, after her mother's death, Jing-mei sits down at the piano and learns a lesson about herself, her mother, and her life.*

Prereading

1. Ask the questions below. Then start a discussion by describing a time when you felt forced by your parents to become involved in an activity. Encourage students to share their experiences.
    • As a child, did you ever do something because your parents wanted you to? How did you feel?

2. Read the introduction on page 101 aloud. Discuss what students think the two kinds of daughters might be. List their suggestions.

Active Reading

1. Invite volunteers to read the first two paragraphs aloud. Discuss why Jing-mei's mother reads these stories of amazing children.

2. Let students read the story silently in groups of three or four. After the group has finished a section, have them predict what will happen next and why. Groups should record their predictions, then check and revise them.

3. Have the groups read and discuss the questions on page 117.

Reading Follow-up

Discuss the questions on page 117 with the class. Bring out the following concepts:

• Jing-mei expects to become a prodigy overnight and win her mother's adoration. When she fails at her first few attempts, she becomes impatient and tired of disappointing her mother.

• Jing-mei doesn't improve as a pianist because she doesn't practice, she doesn't care about playing, and her instructor is all but deaf.

• Jing-mei ends the argument by saying that she wishes she were dead like her mother's previous daughters—twins who were killed in China. The mother is broken by the comment.

Reading Comprehension

Recognizing Conflict

Ask students to describe the major conflict in "Two Kinds." Is it internal or external? Review with students external and internal conflicts. (See page 39 ["The White Umbrella"] of this Teacher's Guide.)

Ask students whether either main character suffers from internal conflict. Students should see that Mrs. Woo's conflict seems to be external; she feels that she is doing the right thing. Her daughter, on the other hand, is different. Then ask students whether they think Jing-mei the adult resolved the internal conflict she felt as a child.

Writing

Author's Craft: Point of View

Review with students the two most common points of view. (See page 12 ["Andrew"] in this Teacher's Guide.) Have them identify the point of view in "Two Kinds." (first person) Asking these questions will help them identify the point of view.
• Who is telling the story?
• Do you know what is going on in each character's mind—or just one?

Have students complete the activities on page 117.

Theme Links: Memories

Using the Theme Links

Remind the class that the activities on these pages will help them understand how the selections they have just read will help them think about what makes events memorable and identify some important memories of their own.

All students should take part in a group discussion of the theme and complete the The Theme and You activity. Let students choose one of the remaining Theme Link activities or suggest another activity they would like to work on independently or with a partner or group.

Student Activities

Group Discussion

Encourage students to list additional questions or concepts they would like to discuss. Allow fifteen to twenty minutes for the discussions. Then have groups share their observations with the class.

This Is Your Life

Suggest that students write answers for the questions they develop and make a brief outline for their show. They may also feel more comfortable and prepared if they turn their questions and answers into a script.

Making Memories

You may wish to make this an ongoing class activity by creating a class memory box. Ask all students to contribute ideas and share memorable events with the class.

The Theme and You

Because some of the students' memories will be very personal, encourage only those students who volunteer to share their letters with the class. You may want to introduce this writing activity by listing several common childhood memories and discussing them with the class.

Checking Theme Goals

Have students refer to the goals they set at the beginning of this unit. Discuss their goals and outcomes with the class. Ask them to explain what they think their memories tell about them. Also ask how these memories will help future generations understand what this time was like.

Unit 4: Surprises

Building Background

What is a surprise? Discuss with the class some of the surprises they have experienced. Point out that surprises can be pleasant or unpleasant. Encourage students to talk about what kinds of things might surprise someone and how different kinds of surprises make people feel. Record their ideas in a cluster diagram like the one below.

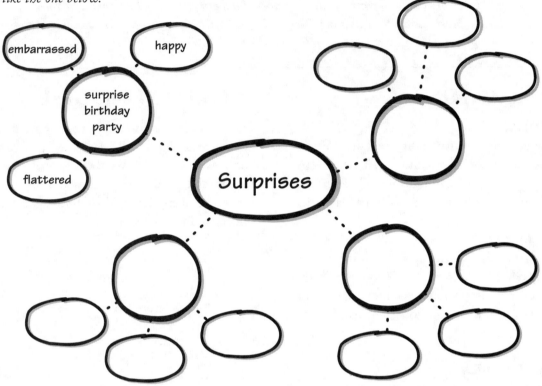

Previewing

Have students read and discuss the unit contents on page vii. Discuss the kinds of selections they will be reading and ask how they think each selection might relate to the theme.

Then discuss the illustration on pages 120 and 121. Ask students what kind of surprise they think each part of the illustration might represent. Add any new ideas to the cluster diagram.

Reading and Discussion

Have students read the unit introduction silently. Then call on volunteers to read each paragraph aloud. Use questions like the following to guide a discussion.

- What kinds of surprising situations came to mind after reading this introduction?

- Who would like to describe a situation when you were surprised? How did the surprise make you feel? What did you learn from this experience?

Setting Theme Goals

Help students set their own goals for reading the selections and understanding the theme. Goals might include the following:

- to read about different kinds of surprises

- to compare what a character does when surprised with what I might do in those circumstances

- to read and enjoy interesting stories and poems

Tell students to write at least two goals in their notebooks. Remind them that they will refer to these goals after they have read the unit selections.

My Sister Ate an Orange

Jack Prelutsky

Poem Summary

A speaker uses multiple meanings of the word orange *(the color of a crayon; the fruit) to trick readers into thinking that his sister ate a piece of fruit when, in fact, she ate four crayons—an orange, a yellow, a purple, and a blue.*

Prereading

1. Ask students to start a list on the board of the strangest things their siblings have eaten. Have them explain the circumstances and describe how the child and others reacted.

2. Have a volunteer read the introduction on page 122 aloud. Ask students what they think might be the surprise in this poem.

Active Reading

1. Give students time to read the poem silently several times—first for general meaning, then to appreciate the rhyme and rhythm, and finally, for fluency and enjoyment. Then call on several volunteers to read the poem aloud.

2. Have students think about the answers to the questions on page 123.

Reading Follow-up

Discuss the questions on page 123 with the class. Bring out the following concepts:

• Students will probably say that at first they thought the sister ate an orange—a piece of fruit—because oranges taste good and people usually don't eat crayons.

• The sister eats an orange crayon.

• At first the speaker is astonished, but after thinking about it, he realizes that it is quite a novel thing to do.

Reading Comprehension

Vocabulary: Multiple Meaning Words

Invite a volunteer to explain what makes the last stanza so surprising. Students should understand that the poet is using multiple meanings to trick readers into thinking that the sister is eating an orange—a kind of fruit—when she's actually eating an orange-colored crayon. Remind students that a word may have several different meanings.

Invite students to think of other multiple meaning words. Write their responses on the board. Encourage students to think of funny situations in which they could use a multiple meaning word to create a surprise.

Writing

Author's Craft: Rhythm and Rhyme

Remind students that the rhyme scheme of a poem is the pattern of rhyming words. The rhythm of a poem is the pattern of stressed and unstressed syllables that repeat to give the poem its beat. Point out that rhythm and rhyme help make poems fun to read and easy to remember.

Have students reread the poem and identify the rhyme scheme (last word in the second and fourth lines rhyme).

Have students apply what they know about rhyming as they work on the activities on page 123.

Speed Cleen
J a m e s   S t e v e n s o n

Story Summary

Harry Joe Shreve leaves the turnpike to use a car wash in a run-down area of a town that he's never been in before. He treats the attendants rudely, then watches his car go into the Speed Cleen Car Wash—but he doesn't see it come out. The surprise ending reveals that Shreve's car was quickly disassembled for parts after entering the car wash. The car-wash attendants are running a chop shop.

Prereading

1. Ask the prereading questions below. Discuss troublemakers that students have known.
   - *Do you know people who cause problems for themselves because of the way they treat others?*
   - *What does the saying "That person's just asking for trouble" mean to you?*

2. Read the introduction on page 124 aloud. What strange things might happen at a car wash?

Active Reading

1. Have a student read the first paragraph aloud. What do students think will happen to Harry Joe Shreve's car? Why? List the predictions.

2. Give students time to read the story silently. Then ask them to prepare sections of the text and take turns reading the story aloud. Help students visualize the setting as they read about it. On the board, map the car wash, auto-parts store, and turnpike.

3. Have students think about the answers to the questions on page 130.

Reading Follow-up

Discuss the questions on page 130 with the class. Bring out the following concepts:

- At the beginning of the story, Shreve scolds an attendant for failing to remove a "V-shaped smear that looked like oil" from the left headlight of the Chrysler. After Shreve's car is missing, Shreve peers through the window of a nearby auto-parts store and sees a headlight with a small V-shaped black smear on the rim. Apparently Shreve's car was disassembled inside the car wash, and the parts were moved to a nearby auto-parts store.

- Shreve is rude and arrogant toward the attendants. He calls one "boy," and he grabs the other to point out the oil spot on the headlight.

- The attendants decide not to give Shreve a ticket because of his rude behavior.

Reading Comprehension
Predict Outcomes

Remind students that making predictions will help them understand what they read and that predictions should be based on story information as well as their own experiences. Discuss the predictions students made after reading the first paragraph of "Speed Cleen." Then ask what predictions they made later in the story. List the story details that led to these predictions and the information from their personal experiences that helped students make the predictions. Invite students to discuss why their predictions were wrong or how the story surprised them.

Writing
Author's Craft: Foreshadowing

Remind students that authors use foreshadowing to prepare a reader for an event or action later in the story. Foreshadowing consists of hints or bits of information given by the narrator that let the reader know what is to come.

Ask students to find examples of foreshadowing in the story and to explain what each example hints at.

Allow time for students to work on the writing activities on page 130.

Unfolding Bud

N a o s h i   K o r i y a m a

Poem Summary

A speaker compares a water lily's blossoming to the gradual blossoming of a poem. At first glance, the poem seems "tight-closed," but on subsequent readings, it slowly opens to reveal its beauty and meaning.

Prereading

1. Start a discussion by talking about a time when your understanding of a poem deepened after you read it several times. Ask students what kinds of poems they like and why. Do they enjoy poetry that rhymes or has a marked rhythm, or do they prefer free verse?

2. Many people have never seen a water lily. To help set the stage for "Unfolding Bud," show students pictures of the flower. (Monet's *Water-Lily Pool* is one example.)

Active Reading

1. Give students time to read the poem silently. Then call on several volunteers to read the poem aloud. Ask students to compare their poetry-reading experiences with the poet's.

2. Have students read the questions on page 132 silently and think about the answers.

Reading Follow-up

Discuss the questions on page 132 with the class. Elicit the following concepts:

- The speaker is describing the blossoming of a water-lily bud into a flower. The event is amazing to the speaker because the bud is transformed into a thing of great beauty.

- In the second stanza, the poet compares a hastily read poem to a tightly closed bud. In the third stanza, the poet compares the gradual understanding of a poem's meaning to the blossoming of a flower.

- The similarity among the first lines of the stanzas ("One is amazed," "One is not amazed," "Yet one is surprised") establishes a pattern and helps readers follow the comparison. The first line of stanza 2 and the first line of stanza 3 act as transitions.

Reading Comprehension

Rereading

Ask students to tell why they like listening to their favorite songs again and again or why they enjoy watching good movies more than once. Point out that one strategy that can help them gain a deeper understanding and appreciation of literature is rereading. Reading a poem a second, third, or fourth time often reveals aspects about it that a person missed the first time he or she read it.

Encourage students to reread "Unfolding Bud." Invite volunteers to share any revelations, thoughts, or questions they have after this reading.

Writing

Poet's Craft: Metaphor and Simile

Remind students that a simile is a direct comparison in which one thing is said to be like something else. A simile uses the word *like* or *as*. A metaphor is a comparison that illustrates a similarity between two people, places, or things by saying that one thing is the other.

Clarify the difference between the two types of comparisons by writing the following on the board:
- simile: A poem is as tight-closed as a tiny bud.
- metaphor: A poem is a water-lily bud.

Allow time for students to complete the writing activities on page 132.

Through a Glass Darkly

Bill Cosby

Selection Summary

Comedian Bill Cosby describes a time when his glasses "disappeared." After looking all over the house, Cosby is sure that either his children or his wife is responsible for the missing glasses. Entering a bathroom, Cosby catches sight of himself in the mirror and of something sitting on top of his head—his glasses—right where he had pushed them.

Prereading

1. Discuss with the class what it means to be absentminded. Tell about a time when you absentmindedly did something funny. Have students share similar stories of their own.

2. Read the introduction on page 133 aloud. Discuss what students think the selection will be about and help them set a goal for reading.

Active Reading

1. Allow time for students to read the selection silently in small groups. Then have group members read the selection aloud as a recorder maps out Cosby's route on a floor plan of his house.

2. Have the groups discuss the answers to the questions on page 136.

Reading Follow-up

Discuss the questions with the class and bring out the following concepts:

• Cosby cannot find his glasses because he usually doesn't push his glasses to the top of his head.

• Cosby blames his children and his wife because he doesn't believe that he could be so absentminded as to lose his glasses.

• Bill Cosby is a very funny person. He is proud but also humble enough to make fun of his own quirkiness or shortcomings.

Reading Comprehension

Personal Experience

Point out that everybody at one time or another has misplaced something. That is one reason this piece is effective. Readers identify with Cosby by recalling similar experiences. Invite students to describe the

thoughts and feelings people have while searching for a misplaced item. Let students ask these questions:

• How are my experiences similar to or different from the speaker's?

• Does the speaker describe feelings and actions that parallel my own experiences?

• What do my experiences add to my understanding or appreciation of the essay?

You might read the essay again, encouraging students to point out passages that remind them of their personal experiences.

Writing

Author's Craft: Hyperbole/Exaggeration

Define hyperbole as extravagant exaggeration used to make a point. Explain that writers expect readers to know that exaggerations are not to be taken literally. Ask students to locate exaggerations in the selection. Possible answers include

• children circling the desk like vultures around a dying zebra

• the friend calling to ask about dried-up felt markers

• Cosby leaving insect spray in the refrigerator

• Cosby explaining that he knows where every atom in his office is

Ask students for examples of hyperbole or exaggeration they have heard or used, or suggest that they make up their own by describing common objects, situations, or events in an exaggerated fashion.

Students should keep these points about hyperbole in mind as they work on the writing activities on page 136.

The Right Kind of House

Henry Slesar

Story Summary

When Mr. Waterbury arrives in Ivy Corners looking for a house to buy, the only one that interests him belongs to elderly Sadie Grimes. The house is ridiculously overpriced. Why is Waterbury willing to pay the price? The mystery is solved when Sadie tells him of her son, a thief who was murdered by his accomplice for hiding a large sum of money they had stolen. Since her son's death, Sadie has sought vengeance on the unknown accomplice. The price is a trap she has set. Only the accomplice would be willing to pay it, because he knows the house contains stolen money. Waterbury is her man, and Sadie poisons him.

Prereading

1. Ask the prereading questions below. Discuss how people gather clues when they read or view a mystery story. Ask students for examples from their experience.
   - *What do you like about mystery stories?*
   - *What are some mysteries you've read or seen?*

2. Read the introduction on page 137 aloud. Discuss possible answers to the questions. Then have students read to find out the real answers.

Active Reading

1. Invite volunteers to read the first two paragraphs aloud. Encourage students to predict what they think will happen and why.

2. Have students prepare and then take turns reading the story aloud. Ask the rest of the class to follow along in their books, listening carefully for clues that might solve the mystery of the house's high price. Each time a clue is read, students should say "Stop!" List the clues.

3. Have students read the questions on page 149 silently and think about the answers.

Reading Follow-up

Discuss the questions on page 149 with the class. Bring out the following concepts:

- Hacker believes Sadie is so sentimental about the house that she has put a high price on it to prevent its sale. However, the high price is a trap for her son's murderer.

- Mr. Waterbury knows that Michael Grimes hid the stolen money in the house.

- The lemonade tastes bitter because Sadie has put poison in it.

Reading Comprehension

Understand Character

Stories contain two major types of characters—flat and round. Flat characters are one-dimensional. They do not undergo any psychological changes as a result of their experiences. Their behavior is predictable. Round characters are more fully developed; they change as a result of their experiences.

Let students skim the story and list details about the characters, which are one-dimensional and flat. If the characters were more rounded, they might seem real, and the dark humor of the story would seem inappropriate.

Writing

Author's Craft: Plot

Explain that plot is the sequence of events in a story. (See page 27 of this Teacher's Guide for more information on plot.) Character and plot are closely related: without characters there is no plot; without a plot, characters are static.

To develop a plot, students can use the same questions they ask when examining a plot:
- Who is the main character?
- What is his or her problem?
- What important events might happen?
- How will the character solve the problem?

Have students write another scene between Michael Grimes and Waterbury. Have students complete the activities on page 149.

Theme Links: Surprises

Using the Theme Links

The activities on this page will help students make connections between the selections they have just read and discussed and their own lives.

All students should participate in a group discussion of the theme and complete the The Theme and You activity. Let students choose one of the remaining Theme Link activities, or encourage them to suggest another activity they would like to work on independently or with a partner or group.

Student Activities

Group Discussion

Encourage group members to list additional questions or concepts they would like to discuss. Allow fifteen to twenty minutes for the discussions. Then have groups share their observations with the class.

Different Endings

If your students have created a "Class Choice" bulletin board for different endings (see TG page 31, "Different Endings"), you may wish to videotape or photograph a few scenes of one or several of the role-plays and add them to the display.

Made for TV

Students may work with partners or a group to create their ads. Suggest that they study real TV guide ads to get ideas. Remind them that the art should convey mystery or suspense without giving away the ending.

The Theme and You

Remind students that surprises can be funny or scary or intriguing. Encourage those who wish to do so to share their writing with the class.

Checking Theme Goals

Have students look over the goals they set at the beginning of this unit. Discuss their goals and outcomes with the class. Ask students what kinds of surprises they might add to the cluster diagram they worked on before reading the unit.

JAMESTOWN PUBLISHERS

Themes *in* Reading

VOLUME 3

Robert Fulghum

Pat Mora

Ann Cameron

Amy Ling

Gwendolyn Brooks

Esmeralda Santiago

Dave Barry

Julius Lester

and others

A MULTICULTURAL COLLECTION

Contents

Unit 1: Expressions of Love

Building Background

Invite students to give definitions of love. Encourage them to share their ideas about love. Record their thoughts in an idea chart.

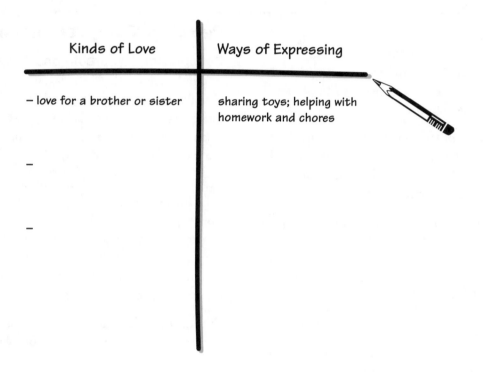

Kinds of Love | Ways of Expressing

– love for a brother or sister | sharing toys; helping with homework and chores

–

–

Previewing

Have students read and discuss the unit contents on page iv. Ask what kinds of selections they will be reading and how they think each selection might relate to the theme. Then discuss the illustration on page 3. Have students study the illustration and describe how each part of the illustration relates to love. Add any new ideas to the idea chart.

Reading and Discussion

Have students read the unit introduction silently. Invite volunteers to read each paragraph aloud. Use questions like the following to guide a discussion.

- How did this introduction change your ideas of what love is?

- Who would like to describe how you express your love to a family member or friend? How does that person respond to your love? How does it make you feel?

Setting Theme Goals

Help students set their own goals for reading the selections and understanding the theme. Goals might include the following:

- to read about different kinds of love

- to share and discuss common emotions and experiences with love

- to read interesting stories and poems

- to think about and understand one's own feelings of love

Tell students to develop at least two goals and write them in their notebooks. Explain that they will return to these goals after they have read the unit selections.

When I Hear Your Name

Gloria Fuertes

Poem Summary

A speaker expresses powerful emotions for a loved one in a series of hyperboles involving the loved one's name. Addressing that special person, the speaker vows to spend eternity repeating the person's name.

Prereading

1. Ask these prereading questions.
   - *Have you ever had such strong feelings for someone that he or she was all you could think about?*
   - *What did you do about it?*

   Then start a discussion by talking about a time when you had strong feelings—positive or negative—for someone. Encourage students to share their experiences.

2. Have a volunteer read the poem title on page 4 aloud. Ask students to take turns completing the sentence. (When I hear your name, I think of riding roller coasters!) Then read the introduction aloud.

Active Reading

1. Give students time to read the poem silently or ask a student to read the poem aloud with feeling, as if he or she were speaking the poem to a loved one.

2. Have students read the Think Back questions on page 6 silently and think about the answers.

Reading Follow-up

Discuss the questions on page 6 with the class. Bring out the following concepts:

- Virtually every statement in the poem is a hyperbole, or extravagant exaggeration.

- Given the speaker's overwhelming love, it's likely she would welcome the sentence.

Reading Comprehension

Recognizing Hyperbole and Exaggeration

Remind students that extravagant exaggeration used to make a point is called hyperbole. Ask students to locate examples of hyperbole in the selection. Have students tell how their impressions of the poem or the speaker are affected by the hyperbole.

Begin a discussion about how authors use hyperbole. Invite volunteers to give some examples of stories, poems, or articles that include hyperbole. Be sure the list includes tall tales, folk tales, and humorous pieces. Point out that hyperbole is often used to create humor. The speaker of this poem uses hyperbole to show the intensity of her feelings.

Encourage students to share examples of hyperbole or exaggeration they have heard or used.

Writing

Author's Craft: Imagery

Remind students that imagery refers to descriptive details that appeal to one or more of the five senses. Vivid imagery includes words that create mental images and evoke our memories of events and objects.

Because the imagery in "When I Hear Your Name" appeals primarily to the sense of sound, invite students to try rewriting the poem, using images that appeal to the other senses.

Have students keep these points in mind as they work on the writing activities on page 6.

The Good Stuff

Robert Fulghum

Selection Summary

Author Robert Fulghum recounts the time when his young daughter Molly gave him a bag filled with odds and ends. Not realizing the significance of the items, Fulghum threw away the bag at work. When his daughter asked for the bag, Fulghum realized that the items were more important than he had thought. He quickly returned to work to retrieve the bag from the garbage. Later, Molly explained the significance of each item, and Fulghum came to appreciate Molly's true act of love: she had given him her prized treasures to care for.

Prereading

1. Have students make a list of gifts people might give to others. Next to each gift, invite students to describe the significance of the item. Example: a diamond ring signifies love or an engagement to be married.

2. Ask a student to read the introduction on page 7 aloud. Discuss what students think the selection will be about, and help them set a purpose for reading.

Active Reading

1. Read the first three paragraphs aloud. Have students describe Robert Fulghum's personality and predict what he might do with the bag.

2. Have students read the selection silently and discuss it in small groups. Suggest that they stop at appropriate points to discuss the text or to discuss a group member's question.

3. Have students read the questions on page 12 silently and think about the answers.

Reading Follow-up

Discuss the questions on page 12 with the class. Bring out the following concepts:

• The items in the bag are Molly's favorite things. They all have special memories associated with them.

• After he learns the significance of the items in the bag, Fulghum considers the bag a Daddy Prize. He tries to be good so that Molly might give it to him again.

• The bag of items is a symbol of his daughter's affection.

Reading Comprehension

Compare and Contrast

Comparing and contrasting helps readers understand characters, situations, settings, and events more vividly by seeing how they are similar or different. To help students gain a deeper understanding and appreciation of Fulghum's experience, create a compare and contrast chart on the board. On the left side of the chart, write students' descriptions of Fulghum before he learned the significance of Molly's bag. On the right side, write students' descriptions of Fulghum at the end of the selection. Have students discuss how Fulghum changed.

Writing

Author's Craft: Tone

Tone is an author's attitude toward his or her subject. The author's choice of words, details, and descriptions of characters and events determine the tone.

Point out that authors sometimes use several tones to show a change in character or personality. Ask students to identify the tone in the selection. Possible answers include condescending, humbling, thankful. Have students identify words or phrases that helped them describe the tone.

Have students focus on how to convey tone as they work on the writing activities on page 12.

Los Ancianos

Pat Mora

Poem Summary

A speaker watches and describes an elderly couple as they walk through a crowded plaza. The speaker is taken by the way the couple are dressed and by the way their actions reflect their love for each other.

Prereading

1. Ask these questions. Then start a discussion about old couples that students know.
   - *Would you like to be married to the same person for fifty years? Why or why not?*
   - *In what ways do a man and woman change after many years of marriage?*

2. Explain that the title, "Los Ancianos," means *the old people* in Spanish. Invite a student to read the introduction on page 13 aloud. What do students think the poem will be about?

Active Reading

1. Give students time to read the poem silently. Then have them take turns reading the poem aloud.

2. Have students read the questions on page 14 silently and think about the answers.

Reading Follow-up

Discuss the questions on page 14 with the class. Elicit the following concepts:

- The speaker knows that the old couple are in love because they hold hands as they walk and the old man helps the woman off the curb.

- The old man and woman differ from the people around them in the way they move through the plaza and in their dress.

Reading Comprehension

Generate Questions

Ask students to describe parts of the poem that confuse or interest them, or leave them wanting to know more. Point out that one way to gain a better understanding and appreciation of a poem is to ask questions about it.

Help students generate questions by sharing your own questions about the poem. Some questions you might ask include the following:
- Where is the old couple going?
- Are the old man and woman tourists too?
- What is the speaker doing in the plaza? Is he or she alone?
- Is the speaker in love with somebody at the moment?

Invite students to share and discuss their questions about "Los Ancianos." Encourage them to try to answer each other's questions.

Writing

Poet's Craft: Simile and Metaphor

Remind students that a simile is a direct comparison of two unlike things using the word *like* or *as*. Point out that a metaphor is an indirect comparison that illustrates a similarity between two unlike things.

Clarify the difference between similes and metaphors by writing the following examples on the chalkboard. Discuss each comparison.
- simile: I could smell love like dried flowers.
- metaphor: Careful together they cross the plaza both slightly stooped, aging trees bending in the wind, returning to the land.

Suggest to students that they keep the distinction between similes and metaphors in mind as they work on the writing activity on page 14.

Mark Messner

Mitch Albom

Selection Summary

Sportswriter Mitch Albom describes the touching relationship of professional football player Mark Messner and his stepfather. A child of divorce, Mark Messner had one constant in his life—his stepfather, Del Pretty. Even after Mark's mother and Del divorced, Del was a continuing influence on Mark. When Del was first diagnosed with lymph node cancer, he beat it into remission for a time. However, the cancer returned. Albom graphically describes the effects of chemotherapy on Del's body and how Mark tenderly and faithfully took care of his dying stepfather.

Prereading

1. Start a discussion about families by telling about a family member who is very important to you. Encourage students to describe ways they and a special family member show love for one another.

2. Read the introduction on page 15 aloud. Discuss students' impressions of professional football players. Then help them set a purpose for reading.

Active Reading

1. Call on volunteers to read the first three paragraphs aloud. Ask students to predict what they think will happen and why. Write their predictions on the chalkboard.

2. Have students skim the text to find unfamiliar medical terms. Define these unfamiliar words or phrases before students read the selection silently.

3. Have students read the questions on page 23 silently and think about the answers.

Reading Follow-up

Discuss the questions on page 23 with the class. Bring out the following concepts:

• Mark Messner's family life was unstable. Del Pretty, his stepfather, is the one constant in his life.

• Del Pretty influences Mark Messner by teaching him about family responsibilities, by answering his questions about life, and by providing an example of determination.

• Mark Messner takes on the role of father to his dying stepfather by taking care of him throughout Del's illness.

Reading Comprehension

Cause and Effect

Explain that a cause is an event or action that directly results in another event or action—the effect. Students will be better readers if they recognize that specific events, actions, and character motives are causes for other events and actions. Words and phrases such as *because, therefore, so,* and *as a result* signal cause and effect relationships.

Have students find cause and effect relationships in "Mark Messner." Write their findings on the chalkboard.

Writing

Author's Craft: Chronological Order

Remind students that when they write about a series of events, they should describe those events in chronological order—the order in which they happened.

Ask students to list in chronological order on the chalkboard the progression of Del Pretty's battle against cancer. Remind students that words such as *first, second, next, before, after, then,* and *finally* are signal words that help writers present a series of events in logical progression.

Remind students to use transition words as they work on the writing activities on page 23.

Mother

B e a   E x n e r   L i u

Poem Summary

A daughter returns to her mother's home after the parent dies. As the daughter walks through the house, she wishes she could see her mother one more time. The daughter seems to hear the mother's voice as she sits next to her empty chair.

Prereading

1. To start a discussion, describe the loss of someone close to you and how you felt about it. Ask students to describe similar events in their own lives.

2. Have a student read the introduction on page 24 aloud. Discuss what students might wish for in that situation. Help them set a purpose for reading.

Active Reading

1. Tell students to think about the speaker's feelings toward her mother and her mother's death as they read the poem silently. Then have volunteers read the poem aloud.

2. Have students read the questions on page 26 silently and think about the answers.

Reading Follow-up

Discuss the questions on page 26 with the class. Bring out the following concepts:

• The daughter thinks of what she and her mother would do if they could be together one more time and of all the things that she misses about her mother.

• The daughter most misses talking about her problems with her mother. Note that the poem opens with the line "I wish that I could talk with her again" and ends with the daughter's imagining her mother speaking with her.

• For most of the poem, the tone is sad. The feeling expressed in the last line, however, is different. The speaker seems encouraged by the advice she imagines her mother giving her, and the tone is upbeat and optimistic.

Reading Comprehension

Recognize Transitions

Explain to students that a transition is a word or group of words that connects ideas and shows logical relationships. Point out that the first line in the second stanza acts as a transition from the speaker's wishful thinking described in the first stanza to the harsh reality described in the second stanza.

To help students see the importance of the transition, invite a student to read the first two stanzas aloud, omitting the transition. Students should see that without the transition, the shift in ideas is difficult to follow.

Writing

Author's Craft: Theme

Remind students that the theme is the underlying idea or message in a poem. Usually the theme of a poem does not teach; it helps us understand life and often raises more questions. Point out that in poetry, the theme is usually not stated directly. A reader must figure out what the author is trying to say. To help students examine the theme in a poem or story, suggest that they first identify the major conflict that the main character or speaker is grappling with.

Have volunteers suggest statements of theme for "Mother." Possible answers include "One must accept reality," "It is important to move on in one's life," and "We should express thoughts and feelings to those we love before it's too late."

Students should think about the theme of the poem as they work on the writing activities on page 26.

The Night We Started Dancing

Ann Cameron

Story Summary

Luisito, a young Guatemalan boy, tells about the Christmas that changed his grandfather's life. Three years previously, Luisito's parents died in a bus accident. Everyone had accepted their death except Luisito's grandfather. He didn't want anyone to talk about Luisito's parents or to celebrate Christmas. After several years, Luisito's grandmother, aunts, and uncles threaten to celebrate Christmas without the grandfather. Luisito's grandfather finally agrees to participate in the celebration. In the course of the night, he comes to accept the death of Luisito's parents, the acceptance symbolized by his dancing.

Prereading

1. Students can recall the prereading discussion for the poem "Mother" about their experience with the loss of a loved one. Start a chart that lists the feelings people have when a loved one dies and ways to cope with the grief.

2. Read the introduction on page 27 aloud. What one word indicates that the story might tell about an unhappy event? (*overshadowed*)

Active Reading

1. Invite volunteers to read the first two paragraphs aloud. Have students predict what they think will happen and why.

2. Allow time to read the story silently. You may also assign students to prepare and read the roles of the characters in the story.

3. Encourage students to compare the way Luisito's grandfather acts after the death of his son and daughter-in-law with the way the speaker in "Mother" acts. Then have students read the questions on page 43 silently and think about the answers.

Reading Follow-up

Discuss the questions on page 43 with the class. Bring out the following concepts:

- Luisito is proud of his Quiché heritage. One can tell by his negative descriptions of the Spaniards and their defeat of the Quichés.

- The grandfather doesn't respect his own father because he spent most of his time drinking and spending the family's money.

- Luisito's grandfather agrees to celebrate Christmas because his family threatens to celebrate without him. He dances because he finally comes to accept the deaths.

Reading Comprehension

Understand Character

Ask students to describe Luisito's grandfather and to tell what happens to him in the course of the story. Remind students that stories may contain two types of characters—flat and round. Flat characters are one-dimensional. They do not undergo any psychological changes as a result of their experiences, and their behavior is very predictable. Round characters are more fully developed, and they change as a result of their experiences. Students should see that Luisito's grandfather is a round character. His actions are difficult to predict, and he undergoes a psychological change. Ask students to decide whether the other characters in the story are round or flat.

Writing

Author's Craft: Flashback

A flashback is an interruption of a story's narrative in which the writer presents an earlier scene or episode. Flashbacks are often crucial to understanding a story because they introduce information that would otherwise be unavailable.

Ask students to reread the flashback and to list the important information it supplies. Have students remember the purpose of a flashback as they work on the writing activities on page 43.

Theme Links: Expressions of Love

Using the Theme Links

Explain to the class that the activities on these pages will help them make connections between the selections they have just read and discussed and their own lives.

All students should participate in a group discussion of the theme and complete the The Theme and You activity. Let students choose one of the remaining Theme Link activities or suggest another activity they would like to work on independently or with a partner or group.

Student Activities

Group Discussion

Encourage students to develop additional questions or concepts they would like to discuss. Allow fifteen to twenty minutes for the discussions. Then have groups share their observations with the class.

Meet the Characters

Students can ask school counselors, teachers, or other respected and knowledgeable people to review their advice. Feedback received may be more meaningful if students provide reviewers with some background on the character and selection they choose.

Songs of Love

Suggest that students compile the love songs on an audiotape to create an album. Have them create a cover for the album and title and credits pages. Students might also enjoy writing liner notes for the album.

The Theme and You

Help students understand that love is a very personal emotion and that it is natural for people to be hesitant about sharing their feelings.

Checking Theme Goals

Have students refer to the goals they noted at the beginning of this unit. Discuss their goals and outcomes with the class. Ask what they might add to the idea chart they worked on before reading the unit.

Unit 2: Special People

Building Background

Discuss with the class what makes a person special. Encourage students to describe special people they know. Record their ideas on a page of Who's Who of Special People.

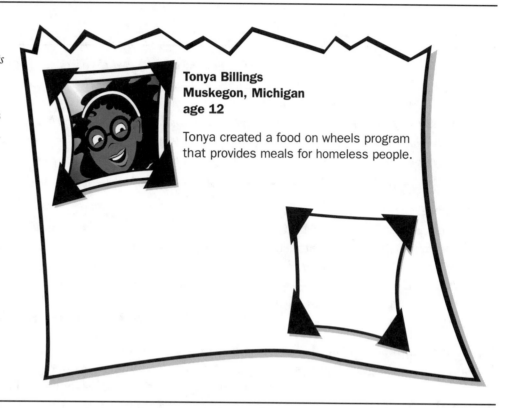

**Tonya Billings
Muskegon, Michigan
age 12**

Tonya created a food on wheels program that provides meals for homeless people.

Previewing

Have students read and discuss the unit contents on page v. Encourage them to talk about what kinds of selections they will be reading and how they think each selection might relate to the theme.

Discuss the illustration on pages 46 and 47. Ask students to describe the people in the illustration and to discuss who they might be. Add any new ideas or features to the *Who's Who of Special People* book.

Reading and Discussion

Have students read the unit introduction silently. Then invite volunteers to read each paragraph aloud. Use questions like the following to help guide the discussion.

- In what ways did this introduction change your ideas of what makes a person special?

- How do you determine if a person is special?

- Describe some people you know who fit your definition of special.

Setting Theme Goals

Help students set their own goals for reading the selections and understanding the theme. Goals might include the following:

- to read about people who are special for a variety of reasons

- to learn about some of the special people in history

- to read interesting stories and poems

- to learn from and be inspired by the special people in the selections

Tell students to write at least two goals in their notebooks. Explain that they will return to these goals after they have read the unit selections.

Grandma Traub and Grandma Ling

Amy Ling

Poem Summaries

"Grandma Traub" describes Ling's maternal grandmother, who adopted the poet's mother when her mother died in China. Big, bold, and strong, Grandma Traub helped raise the speaker in Pennsylvania and endeared herself to her adopted grandchildren because of the special care she gave them. In "Grandma Ling," poet Amy Ling describes her paternal grandmother, who shares the poet's Chinese physical features. Grandma Ling lives in Taiwan and speaks a language the poet cannot understand, but they share and understand the special ties of family.

Prereading

1. Ask these questions. Then start a discussion about grandparents and other relatives.
   - *Does a grandparent (or parent) have to be a blood relative?*
   - *What benefits are there to having two very different grandmothers?*

2. Read the introduction aloud. Ask students to predict what the grandmothers are like.

Active Reading

1. Give students time to read the poems silently, or ask a student to read the poems aloud and emphasize the emotions in the them.

2. Have students read the questions on page 52 silently and think about the answers.

Reading Follow-up

Discuss the questions on page 52 with the class. Bring out the following concepts:

- Grandma Traub is a large, white-haired woman who wears full dresses adorned with jewelry. She is an American who was at one time a missionary nurse and hospital administrator. She was also a good cook and seamstress. Physically, Grandma Ling is very much like Amy Ling, the poet. She is small, with sturdy legs and feet. She has a square forehead, high cheeks, and wide-set eyes. She lives in Taiwan and speaks Chinese. Grandma Ling places great importance on her family.

- While director of Yoyang hospital, Grandma Traub adopted Amy's orphaned mother.

- Grandma Traub's most endearing qualities are the ways she shows her love for her Chinese grandchildren: by cooking special dishes, by reading to them, and by sewing for them.

Reading Comprehension

Rereading

Rereading is a strategy that can help readers gain a deeper understanding and appreciation of a poem. Reading a poem a second, third, or fourth time often reveals aspects of it that readers miss at first.

Share with students things you noticed about "Grandma Traub" or "Grandma Ling" after rereading the poems. What revelations, thoughts, or questions do they have after rereading the poems?

Writing

Poet's Craft: Imagery

Remind students that imagery refers to descriptive details that appeal to one or more of the five senses and create mental images.

Because the imagery in "Grandma Traub" and "Grandma Ling" appeals primarily to the sense of sight, have students rewrite passages of the poems, using images that appeal to the other senses.

Encourage students to be aware of their senses as they work on the activities on page 52.

The Education of a Woman Golfer

Nancy Lopez

Selection Summary

Professional golfer Nancy Lopez writes about the special people in her life who have helped her become one of the greatest woman golfers of all time. Her father and Lee Trevino, a fellow Mexican American golfer, are among them.

Prereading

1. Start a concept web about golf, and record the thoughts, feelings, and images that students associate with golf. Then ask these questions.
   - *How is golf different from other professional sports?*
   - *What skills or character traits do many good golfers share?*

2. Students may not be familiar with Nancy Lopez, regarded by many as the greatest woman golfer ever. Born in 1957, she was a legitimate contender in professional tournaments by the time she was eighteen years old. As a professional rookie in 1978, she won nine tournaments. She has won more than forty-five tournaments in her career. In 1987, she was inducted into the LPGA Hall of Fame.

3. Ask a student to read the title on page 53 aloud. What kind of education do students think a woman golfer might need?

Active Reading

1. Have students read the selection silently in small groups, stopping at appropriate points to discuss what they've read or whenever a group member has a question.

2. Have students read the questions on page 57 silently and think about the answers.

Reading Follow-up

Discuss the questions on page 57 with the class. Bring out the following concepts:

- The greatest obstacle Nancy Lopez overcomes to become a good golfer is racism. Because she is Mexican American, many people in her town look down on her and won't let her play on the better local golf courses.

- Lee Trevino teaches Nancy not to be too analytical about her golf game and not to worry about the mechanics of her swing.

- Nancy has mixed feelings about Roswell because she experienced racism there.

Reading Comprehension

Cause and Effect

An autobiography is the story of someone's life written by himself or herself. For the reader to fully understand and appreciate the events in the writer's life, the writer must describe the causes and effects of each event. Remind students that a cause is an event or action that directly results in another event or action—the effect. Explain that terms such as *because, therefore, so,* and *as a result* signal cause and effect relationships.

Have students reread the selection to locate the main events or incidents that Nancy Lopez describes. Ask students to identify the causes and effects of each main event.

Writing

Author's Craft: Direct Quotations

A direct quotation is the exact words of a person. Writers of nonfiction often use direct quotations to support an opinion or idea, to reveal information, to show thoughts and feelings of the person quoted, or to move an account along.

Let students find direct quotations in the selection and explain what each quotation reveals.

Remind students to use quotation marks correctly as they work on the writing activities on page 57.

Grassy's Theme

Jesse Stuart

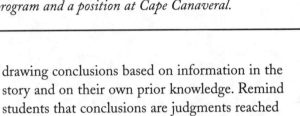

Selection Summary

Author and educator Jesse Stuart tells about Bruce "Grassy" Barnhill, a former student who made a lasting impression on Stuart because of a theme he wrote in Stuart's class involving space, time, and math—Grassy's favorite subjects. Years later, Stuart finds out from Grassy's young cousin that Grassy's interest in space, time, and math led to a career in the space program and a position at Cape Canaveral.

Prereading

1. Ask students the questions below. Then start a discussion about their favorite teachers.
   - *How can a teacher influence a student?*
   - *What advice should teachers give students?*

2. Read the introduction on page 58 aloud. What do students think Grassy might have done?

Active Reading

1. Invite volunteers to read the first two paragraphs aloud. Ask students to give a character description of Grassy Barnhill. Then have students predict Grassy's future.

2. Have students read the questions on page 65 silently and think about the answers.

Reading Follow-up

Discuss the questions on page 65 with the class. Elicit the following concepts:

- Grassy Barnhill is unusual not only because he and his sister walk eight miles to school but because he is interested in math, time, space, and the universe. He puts a lot of time and effort into his schoolwork.

- Grassy doesn't tell anyone about his work in California because he is working on classified scientific projects.

- After learning about Grassy's success, Stuart realizes how important it is to encourage his students and not to inhibit their thinking.

Reading Comprehension

Draw Conclusions

When students described Grassy Barnhill after reading the first two paragraphs, they did so by drawing conclusions based on information in the story and on their own prior knowledge. Remind students that conclusions are judgments reached after thinking about details and using common sense.

Drawing conclusions involves going beyond a selection to put together various text clues. For example, many students may have drawn the conclusion that the reason Grassy's father never knew what kind of work his son did was because Grassy's job was classified. Students can piece together information from the selection, using their personal knowledge of the secrecy of the defense industry to draw that conclusion. Encourage students to draw conclusions about other aspects of the selection.

Writing

Writer's Craft: Dialogue

Author Jesse Stuart describes events that took place many years ago. To help readers understand the events and identify with the people he writes about, Stuart re-creates conversations by using dialogue. Dialogue makes Grassy and the other people more real.

Dialogue is the conversation of characters in a story. Writers use dialogue to move the story along, to reveal information, and to show the thoughts and feelings of characters. Ask students to find examples of dialogue in the story and to explain what each example reveals.

Remind students to use quotation marks before and after each character's exact words as they work on the writing activities on page 65.

Martin Luther King Jr.

Gwendolyn Brooks

Poem Summary

In a series of metaphors, Gwendolyn Brooks describes the brief but bright life of Martin Luther King, Jr. Using imagery, the poet reminds readers of King's efforts and champions his legacy.

Prereading

1. Ask students to start a profile chart on the chalkboard about Martin Luther King, Jr. Have students list everything they know about him.

2. Read the introduction on page 66 aloud. Then read a copy of King's "I Have a Dream" speech. Encourage students to discuss what they think the poem will be about, and help them set a purpose for reading.

Active Reading

1. Read the poem aloud to let students hear the poem's rich language and rhythm. Then invite volunteers to take turns reading the poem aloud, emphasizing the words that Brooks emphasizes in the poem.

2. Have students read the questions on page 67 silently and think about the answers.

Reading Follow-up

Discuss the questions on page 67 with the class. Bring out the following concepts:

• Brooks describes King in a series of metaphors, comparing him to a prose poem, a tragic grace, and warm music.

• Brooks's imagery appeals primarily to the sense of sound and the sense of sight.

Reading Comprehension

Paraphrase

Point out that when reading a poem like "Martin Luther King Jr.," which contains many metaphors and other abstract comparisons, it is often helpful to stop and paraphrase what was just read—to reword the passage to understand it better.

Remind students that a paraphrase is a restatement of the essential ideas of a piece or passage of writing. Recall for students that when paraphrasing parts of an entire poem, they should restate the ideas in prose if they are writing or explain it in their own words if they are speaking. Choose passages from the poem and have students paraphrase them.

Writing

Poet's Craft: Metaphor

Remind students that a metaphor is a comparison in which one thing is said to be something else. A metaphor appeals to the reader's imagination and allows the reader to understand a passage beyond its literal meaning.

Point out that unlike a simile, which uses the word *like* or *as* to make a comparison, a metaphor often uses the words *is, are, was,* or *were.*

Encourage students to identify the metaphors in the poem and rewrite them by making new, interesting comparisons.

Encourage students to be aware of their senses as they create metaphors for the writing activities on page 67.

Opera, Karate, and Bandits

Huynh Quang Nhuong

Story Summary

A narrator recalls stories about his deceased grandmother. Each story illustrates the grandmother's strong spirit, resilience, and eccentricities that held the family together and made the narrator's childhood memorable.

Prereading

1. Begin a discussion by describing a person you miss very much—someone who either has died or has moved away. Describe why you have such fond memories of the person. Then ask students to share similar experiences. You might ask students to recall the prereading discussions for the poem "Mother" and the story "The Night We Started Dancing."

2. Read the introduction on page 68 aloud. Discuss what qualities students think a grandmother should have. Then help them set a purpose for reading.

Active Reading

1. Call on volunteers to read the first three paragraphs aloud. Ask students to describe the grandmother and to share personal experiences about people they know who are like her.

2. Have students read the story silently.

3. Have students read the questions on page 77 silently and think about the answers.

Reading Follow-up

Discuss the questions on page 77 with the class. Bring out the following concepts:

• The eighty-year-old grandmother can still use her own teeth to eat corn on the cob and chew sugar plants. She can walk for more than an hour to market and then walk home.

• Seeing the "Faithful One" on stage first is bad luck because he is always in trouble and it takes him many years to vindicate himself.

• The grandmother takes care of the rascal by hitting him first on his cheekbone with her elbow and then kicking him in the shin, making him lose his balance. She frightens the bandits away by hiding in the dark and shooting her arrows.

Also discuss the following with students:

• Similarities between the way the narrator of this selection feels about the death of his grandmother and the way the speaker of the poem "Mother" feels about her mother's death

• Similarities and differences between Grandma Traub, Grandma Ling, and the grandmother in this selection

Reading Comprehension

Summarize

Explain that one way to better understand and appreciate "Opera, Karate, and Bandits" is to summarize each of the three anecdotes described in the selection. Remind students that a summary is a shortened version of a text put in the reader's own words. A summary includes the most important information—the characters, setting, events, and problems—and helps readers keep track of what happens or what's described.

Have students summarize the three stories within the selection.

Writing

Author's Craft: Character

Ask students to describe the narrator's grandmother. Write their descriptions on the board. Remind students that authors reveal character through the actions, thoughts, and speech (dialogue) of their characters as well as through direct description.

Students can locate passages that reveal what the grandmother was like. Then have students concentrate on the different ways to describe a character as they work on the writing activities on page 77.

Theme Links: Special People

Using the Theme Links

Remind the class that the activities on these pages will help them make connections between the selections they have just read and discussed and their own lives.

All students should participate in a group discussion of the theme and complete the The Theme and You activity. Students may choose one of the remaining Theme Link activities, or they may suggest another activity they would like to work on independently or with a partner or group.

Student Activities

Group Discussion

Encourage students to think of additional questions or concepts they would like to talk about. Allow fifteen to twenty minutes for the discussions. Then have groups share their observations with the class.

Advice from a Panel of Experts

Suggest that students review the selections for information, and if possible, research the lives of the panel members they are portraying. Students can practice their presentations with each other or at home, seeking feedback from family members.

Special People

Students may enjoy seeking input from other classrooms or from family and friends outside the school to make the hall of fame truly inclusive.

The Theme and You

Help students see that there are many kinds of special people and that each individual determines what makes a person special. Invite volunteers to share their biographical sketches with the class.

Checking Theme Goals

Have students look again at the goals they set at the beginning of this unit. Discuss their goals and outcomes with the class. Ask what they might now add to the *Who's Who of Special People* book they worked on before reading the unit.

Unit 3: Food for Thought

Building Background

With the class, discuss the role of food in their lives. Invite students to describe specific foods that have special cultural or personal significance. You might write their ideas and responses on menu charts like those below.

Breakfast Menu

Lunch Menu

Dinner Menu

Dessert Menu

Apple pie is considered the typical American dessert. It often symbolizes American culture.

Previewing

Have students read and discuss the unit contents on page vi. Ask them what kinds of selections they think they will be reading and how they think each selection might relate to the theme.

Then discuss the illustration on page 81. Ask students to discuss anything about the illustration that interests or confuses them. Add any new ideas, headings, or selections to the menu chart.

Reading and Discussion

Have students read the unit introduction silently. Then call on volunteers to read each paragraph aloud. Questions like the following will help guide a discussion.

• How did this introduction change your ideas about food?

• Who has an interesting story about a particular meal or food? What happened? Why is the story so memorable or significant?

Setting Theme Goals

Help students set their own goals for reading the selections and understanding the theme. Goals might include the following:

• to read and learn about foods and customs of cultures other than your own

• to appreciate the part that food plays in family and cultural life

• to consider the associations that food and food-related events have for themselves and others

• to read interesting stories and poems

Tell students to set at least two goals and write them in their notebooks. Explain that they will return to these goals after they have read the unit selections.

How to Eat a Guava

Esmeralda Santiago

Selection Summary

The author describes how seeing a guava in the local grocery store brings back vivid memories of her childhood in Puerto Rico. Guavas grow wild in Puerto Rico, and the author sensuously recounts how she used to eat fresh, raw guavas. She also recalls the last guava she had—the day she left Puerto Rico. She decides not to buy the enticing guavas that return her to her childhood. Instead, she pushes her cart toward "the apples and pears of [her] adulthood . . . "

Prereading

1. Ask these prereading questions and then discuss students' favorite foods.
   - *Other than satisfying your hunger, how else does food affect you?*
   - *Are there foods that you once enjoyed but no longer eat? Explain.*

2. Have a volunteer read the introduction on page 82 aloud. Ask students to describe a guava.

Active Reading

1. Explain that a guava is a yellow pear-shaped tropical fruit. Guavas are processed into jams, jellies, and preserves. Fresh guavas are often eaten raw and may be sliced and served with sugar and cream as a dessert.

2. Have students read the selection silently.

3. Have students read the questions on page 85 silently and think about the answers.

Reading Follow-up

Discuss the questions on page 85 with the class. Bring out the following concepts:

- The author is originally from Puerto Rico and now lives in New York.

- When the author sees the guava in the Shop & Save, it brings back a flood of memories of her childhood, when she and her friends would pick fresh guavas right from the branches.

- Santiago's detailed, sensuous descriptions of guavas reveal her fondness for the fruit. But guavas also represent a time and place that she'll never recapture: her childhood in Puerto Rico.

Reading Comprehension

Identify Theme

Ask students to discuss what "How to Eat a Guava" is about. Remind students that the theme, the central or underlying idea or message in a story or poem, often helps us understand life. To help students examine the theme, suggest that they first identify the major conflict. Students should see that the narrator is coming to terms with her adulthood while keeping alive the carefree days of her childhood in Puerto Rico.

Have volunteers describe the theme in "How to Eat a Guava." Point out that in fiction and in poetry the theme is usually not stated directly. A reader must infer it.

Writing

Writer's Craft: Sensory Details

Remind students that sensory language includes words and phrases that appeal to one or more of the five senses. Authors use specific nouns, action verbs, and interesting adjectives to create sensory language that helps readers experience a scene, character, event, or other aspect of a story or poem.

Ask students to find examples of sensory language in the selection and to explain which sense the language appeals to. Students should have little difficulty finding sensory details that appeal to the sense of taste or touch. Have students rewrite passages, using sensory details that appeal to other senses.

Remind students to be aware of their senses as they work on the activities on page 85.

In My Mother's Kitchen

S h o n t o   B e g a y

Poem Summary

A speaker lovingly describes his mother as she works in her kitchen. Seeing the mother in the kitchen evokes strong emotions and brings back childhood dreams and memories of happy times for the speaker.

Prereading

1. Start a concept web on the board about kitchens. Have students mention all the things they associate with kitchens, including foods, smells, appliances, and feelings.

2. Have a student read the introduction on page 86 aloud. Encourage students to discuss what they think the poem will be about, and help them set a purpose for reading.

Active Reading

1. Read the poem aloud to let students hear the poem's rich language. Then invite volunteers to take turns reading the poem aloud, emphasizing the emotions.

2. Have students read the questions on page 88 silently and think about the answers.

Reading Follow-up

Discuss the questions on page 88 with the class. Bring out the following concepts:

- The house in the poem is located somewhere in the American Southwest. Details that reveal this include the mention of tortillas, sagebrush hills, and Black Mesa.

- The speaker loves his mother. The speaker makes this clear in the descriptions of her: the morning light gives her a halo; her kitchen makes the speaker feel warm; her smiles recall childhood dreams.

- The speaker describes several emotions, including sadness, happiness, respect, love, regret, and nostalgia.

Reading Comprehension

Rereading

Remind students that one strategy that can help them gain a deeper understanding and appreciation of a poem is rereading. Reading a poem a second, third, or fourth time often reveals aspects of it that readers miss at first.

Share with students things you noticed about "In My Mother's Kitchen" after rereading the poem. Have students read the poem again. Invite volunteers to share any revelations, thoughts, or questions they have after this reading.

Writing

Author's Craft: Mood

Ask students to describe how they feel after reading "In My Mother's Kitchen." Remind students that mood is the feeling a reader gets from a poem or story. Writers create a specific mood through their choice of words and by creating images that show how things look, feel, and sound.

Details such as "soot-grayed walls, secretive and blank"; "the morning light gives her a halo"; and "my mother's gentle movements light up dark corners" all contribute to the mood in the poem. Invite students to suggest words that describe the mood of "In My Mother's Kitchen." Students should see that contrasting images create several moods. Although the kitchen is dark, cold, and sparsely furnished, the speaker's mother is warm. She moves in and out of light like a dream, and she is a source of comfort for the speaker.

Have students consider the relationship between imagery and mood as they work on the writing activities on page 88.

A Taste of Korea

Marie G. Lee

Story Summary

Alice is a girl of Korean descent whose mother gave her up for adoption when Alice was a baby. Reverend Larsen and his family adopted Alice and brought her to live with them in the United States. When Alice is invited to eat at the home of a Korean classmate, her interest and curiosity about her Korean heritage are sparked.

Prereading

1. Begin a discussion about various ethnic cuisines by describing your favorite foods. Encourage students to share their thoughts and feelings about ethnic foods they're familiar with. Then ask the following questions.
   - *Are there some foods that you really want to try but are hesitant about? If so, why?*
   - *Is there such a thing as "American food"? What is it, and what does it reveal about Americans?*

2. Ask a student to read the introduction on page 89 aloud. Discuss what students think the selection will be about, and help them set a purpose for reading.

Active Reading

1. Invite volunteers to read the first page aloud. Encourage students to describe Alice.

2. Have students read the story silently.

3. Have students read the questions on page 97 silently and think about the answers.

Reading Follow-up

Discuss the questions on page 97 with the class. Bring out the following concepts:

- Alice's birth mother put her up for adoption and that's all Alice knows about her. The Larsens have adopted Alice, and she calls Mr. and Mrs. Larsen father and mother.

- Both the Lees and the Larsens are caring, generous people. Even though Yoon Jun and his mother are poor, they are very hospitable and share what little food they have with Alice. The Larsens cared enough about Alice to want her to be part of their family.

- Alice respects and admires the Lees because they can make do with so little and yet still be so generous. She also seems to envy them because they represent a link to Korea and to her own past and culture.

Reading Comprehension

Compare and Contrast

Remind students that authors often juxtapose two or more things, persons, events, or stories, in order to emphasize similarities and differences. Remind students that when they compare, they look for similarities; when they contrast, they look for differences.

Ask students to identify some things that are compared and contrasted in "A Taste of Korea." Students should see that Korean foods and the way Koreans eat are compared to and contrasted with American foods and customs. Also, Korean and American lifestyles are compared and contrasted. Discuss how making these comparisons and contrasts can help readers understand Alice better.

Writing

Author's Craft: Point of View

Review with students first-person and third-person points of view. (See page 12 ["Andrew"] in this Teacher's Guide.) Remind students to ask themselves these questions to help identify point of view. Who is telling the story? Do you know what is going on in every character's mind—or in just one character's?

Have students discuss how seeing story events from Alice's perspective affects their opinions of Alice, the Lees, and the Larsens.

Have students remember these points as they work on the writing activities on page 97.

Hold the Sprouts

D a v e   B a r r y

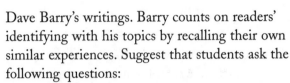

Selection Summary

Columnist Dave Barry pokes fun at the fast-food industry as he describes his plan to make several million dollars in the fast-food business by buying several tons of Brussels sprouts to put in hamburger buns.

Prereading

1. Have students create a list of all the fast-food restaurants they can think of and write the kinds of food the restaurants serve. Have them put stars by the especially good restaurants.

2. Read the introduction on page 98 aloud. Ask students to predict Barry's plan.

Active Reading

1. Allow time for students to read the selection silently, or ask volunteers to read the selection aloud, emphasizing Barry's humorous style.

2. Have students read the questions on page 103 silently and think about the answers.

Reading Follow-up

Discuss the questions on page 103 with the class. Elicit the following concepts:

• Dave Barry thinks fast-food restaurants are successful because they serve foods that only ten-year-olds like and that have high grease and sugar contents.

• Barry, like many people, likes the food at fast-food restaurants, but he is amazed at and perhaps a little appalled with what fast-food restaurants are serving now.

• Barry's plan involves buying several tons of Brussels sprouts, putting them on hamburger buns, and marketing them as fast food.

Reading Comprehension

Personal Experience

Ask students whether they identified with anything in "Hold the Sprouts." Point out that practically everybody in the United States has eaten at a fast-food restaurant. Fast-food restaurants have become a part of American culture—the subject of many of Dave Barry's writings. Barry counts on readers' identifying with his topics by recalling their own similar experiences. Suggest that students ask the following questions:

• How are my experiences similar to or different from the author's?

• Are the author's descriptions of feelings and actions realistic, based on my experiences?

• What do my experiences add to my understanding or appreciation of the essay?

Encourage students to read "Hold the Sprouts" again, noting passages that remind them of their personal experiences.

Writing

Writer's Craft: Hyperbole

Remind students that hyperbole is extravagant exaggeration used to make a point. Writers expect readers to recognize that the exaggerations are not to be taken literally. Ask students to locate the hyperbole in the selection. Possible answers include the following:

• Fast-food restaurants serve food that only ten-year-olds like to eat.

• Milk has been eliminated from milk shakes because the U.S. government has identified milk to be a major cause of nutrition.

• People don't care what they eat as long as it's on a hamburger bun.

• Nobody believes in the Balanced Diet Theory any longer.

Discuss with students Barry's use of hyperbole in this essay and what effect it has on their overall view of the piece. Have students keep these points in mind as they work on the writing activities on page 103.

Stranger at the Table

Bob Greene

Selection Summary

Greene describes how David Gambill and his wife return home from vacation to find an intruder, Allen Young, hiding in a closet. Young, who is homeless, tells Gambill that he broke into the house to feed himself. Greene details the mixed emotions Gambill feels as he allows Young to finish eating before the police arrive. Although Gambill is a victim, his experience opens his eyes to the plight of the homeless and hungry in America.

Prereading

1. Ask these prereading questions. Discuss students' experience with the homeless.
   - *Why are some people homeless?*
   - *Who is responsible for helping the homeless?*

2. Read the introduction on page 104 aloud. What do students think the selection will be about? Help them set a purpose for reading.

Active Reading

1. Read the opening sentence. Ask students to describe their thoughts and feelings after reading this provocative opening.

2. Students can read the selection silently or perform it as a docudrama. Ask one student to read the narrative parts of the selection and other students to read the other lines and perform the actions described.

3. Have students read the questions on page 109 and think about the answers.

Reading Follow-up

Discuss the questions on page 109 with the class. Bring out the following concepts:

- Gambill knows something is wrong because there is food cooking in the kitchen, and he finds that a window has been broken.

- Gambill is afraid and feels threatened and violated. He then feels confused about and saddened by Allen Young's actions.

- The disturbing experience forces Gambill to think about homelessness, a major problem in our society.

Reading Comprehension

Compare and Contrast

Comparing and contrasting helps readers understand characters, situations, settings, and events more vividly and in more detail. Help students gain a deeper understanding of "Stranger at the Table" by asking these questions about Young and Gambill:

- What is each man's lifestyle? (Young is homeless and has to steal food to survive; Gambill owns a home and lives comfortably.)
- Who is the victim, or are both? (Gambill is a victim of crime; Young is possibly a victim of the forces of society.)
- Who shows more emotion? (Gambill is bothered more by the incident because nothing like that has ever happened to him before.)
- Who is more in control of the situation? (Young suggests calling the police instead of trying to escape.)

Writing

Author's Craft: Quotations

Ask students whether the selection would be as compelling if Bob Greene had relied only on police reports to describe the incident. By describing Gambill's reactions, Greene makes the selection more dramatic.

Remind students that a direct quotation is the exact words of a person. Greene uses direct quotations to reveal information and to show Gambill's thoughts and feelings. Have students find quotations in the selection and explain what each reveals. Remind students to enclose quotations in quotation marks as they work on the writing activities on page 109.

Theme Links: Food for Thought

Using the Theme Links

Use the activities on this page to help students make connections between the selections they have just read and discussed and their own lives.

All students should participate in a group discussion of the theme and complete the The Theme and You activity. Let students choose one of the remaining Theme Link activities or suggest another activity they would like to work on independently or with a partner or group.

Student Activities

Group Discussion

Encourage group members to list additional questions or concepts they would like to discuss. Allow fifteen to twenty minutes for the discussions. Then have groups share their observations with the class.

An Interview with Allen Young

Suggest that students watch a professional TV reporter interview a subject or, if possible, meet with a reporter from their community newspaper to help guide their own interviews. Encourage them to get feedback on their questions and responses from classmates, friends, or family members.

Food Chart

You may wish to turn this activity into a live presentation by having students prepare some of the foods on the chart at home with the help of family members. Students can bring in the food to share with the class and provide some background or interesting facts about their selections.

Mouth-Watering Memory

For this activity, have students review the unit selections for examples of sensory language. Encourage students to share their writing with the class if they wish to do so.

The Theme and You

Suggest that students approach the appropriate school administrators or community leaders about putting their action plan to use.

Checking Theme Goals

Have students refer to the goals they set at the beginning of this unit. Discuss their goals and outcomes with the class. Ask what items they might add to the menu chart they worked on before reading the unit.

Unit 4: American History

Building Background

Discuss with the class the importance of studying history. Invite students to talk about important events in United States history. Discuss how this knowledge applies to their own lives. Record their ideas on a time line.

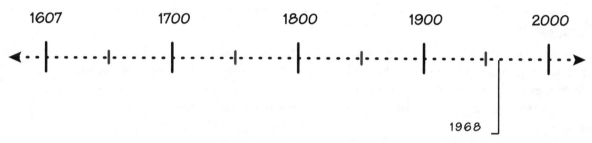

1607   1700   1800   1900   2000

1968
Assassination of Martin Luther King, Jr.
King's example can teach us how to try to
fix problems in our society peacefully.

Previewing

Have students read and discuss the unit contents on page vii. Ask them what kinds of selections they expect to be reading and how they think each selection might relate to the theme. Then discuss the illustration on page 112. Invite students to talk about which events in American history the illustration depicts. Add any new ideas to the timeline.

Reading and Discussion

Have students read the unit introduction silently. Then call on volunteers to read each paragraph aloud. Use questions like the following to guide a discussion.

- How did this introduction change your ideas about how you can learn about history?

- Who can describe a story in which you learned something about American history? What did you learn? Which is more memorable, the story or the historical information?

Setting Theme Goals

Help students set their own goals for reading the selections and understanding the theme. Goals might include the following:

- to read about important periods and people in American history

- to appreciate and understand the accomplishments of Americans who lived before us

- to read and enjoy interesting stories and poems

- to learn how to apply historical knowledge to better our lives and society

Tell students to set at least two goals in their notebooks. Explain that they will refer to these goals after they have read the unit selections.

Letters from the Front

Selection Summary

These letters were written by two Americans who served their country. They are last letters to family members: Sullivan Ballou's letter conveys his feelings about family; his purpose is to write a last letter just in case he dies in battle during the Civil War. Sharon Lane writes of the daily details of working in an army hospital in Vietnam—of injuries and deaths, movies, schedules, and her physical surroundings. Her letter is not written as a final correspondence; she did not expect to die.

Prereading

1. Start a concept web on the board about war by asking students to describe the thoughts and feelings they associate with it. Then have students discuss what they know about the Civil War and the Vietnam War.

2. Have a volunteer read the introductions on pages 114 and 116 aloud. Ask students what they think the letters will be about.

Active Reading

1. Have volunteers read the first two paragraphs of each letter aloud. Ask students to give their impressions of Sullivan Ballou and Sharon Lane.

2. Have students read the letters silently. Then ask volunteers to read the letters aloud, reading Ballou's letter in the formal, sentimental style in which it is written and Lane's letter in the informal, conversational style that characterizes her writing.

3. Have students read the questions on page 119 silently and think about the answers.

Reading Follow-up

Discuss the questions on page 119 with the class. Bring out the following concepts:

• Ballou promises his wife that they will be together after death and that his spirit will always be near her.

• Lane takes her work very seriously. She is aware of statistical information about the number of patients treated, and she knows what happens to many of the patients.

• Ballou's letter is written in case he dies in battle. He also expresses his opinions about the war. Sharon Lane writes of daily details. Her letter is not a final correspondence; she did not expect to die.

Reading Comprehension

Author's Purpose

Encourage students to discuss why Ballou and Lane wrote these letters. Point out to students that just as authors write for specific purposes, so do letter writers. A writer's purpose for writing often determines the reader's purpose. For example, since Ballou's purpose is to write a last letter in case he dies, a reader's purpose might be to find out his emotions.

Ask volunteers to describe Sharon Lane's purpose for writing her letter. What was their purpose for reading it?

Writing

Writer's Craft: Letters

Invite students to describe different types of letters they have written or received. Point out that letters are written to a specific person or audience. The writing style should be appropriate for that audience. For example, a letter written to a Dean of Admissions at a college might have long, formal sentences and would not contain contractions or slang. A letter to a brother or sister away at college would be more conversational in tone, and it might have fragments or slang expressions.

Have students keep their audience in mind as they work on the activities on page 119.

When Freedom Came

Julius Lester

Story Summary

With the Civil War over, Jake, a former slave, is now a free man. He sets out on foot from Pine Bluff, Arkansas, to Pulaski, Tennessee, a trip of more than five hundred miles. Several years before the war ended, Jake's wife and children had been sold to someone else and taken away. After three months on the road, Jake finally finds his wife, Mandy. She tells Jake that she has remarried and that she cannot come back to him.

Prereading

1. Ask students to share what they know about slavery in the United States. Encourage them to discuss the effects slavery had on individuals and their families. Ask students to describe what happened to slaves after the Civil War.

2. Read the introduction on page 120 aloud. What do students think the story will be about? Help them set a purpose for reading.

Active Reading

1. Invite volunteers to read the first paragraph aloud. Encourage students to predict what's going to happen to Jake.

2. Students may have difficulty with the dialect used in the story. Read the story aloud so that students can hear the dialect.

3. Have students read the questions on page 128 silently and think about the answers.

Reading Follow-up

Discuss the questions on page 128 with the class. Bring out the following concepts:

- The main obstacle Jake overcomes is the distance that he has to walk. He also has to stop to work to get money to buy food.

- Ex-slaves found missing loved ones mainly by asking the people they met on the roads if they knew the person.

- Jake is devastated when he realizes that he and Mandy will not be together again. Mandy is saddened but is more accepting and willing to move on with her new life.

Reading Comprehension

Generate Questions

Ask students whether they were disappointed in the ending to "When Freedom Came" and to explain why. Have them discuss parts of the story that confuse, interest, or leave them wanting to know more. When stories have a sad or unexpected ending, readers often try to create meaning and to better understand the story by asking questions about it.

Help students generate and discuss questions about the story. Possible questions include the following:
- Where will Jake go now?
- How could Mandy turn Jake away?
- What do Jake and Mandy's children think about the situation?

Writing

Author's Craft: Dialogue

Remind students that writers use dialogue to move the story along, to reveal information, and to show the thoughts and feelings of characters. Good writers try to capture the way people actually talk. To do this, they often use dialect. A dialect is a form of speech characteristic of a particular region or class, different in some of its words, pronunciations, and grammar from the standard language. Julius Lester captured the dialect of the African American slaves to give readers a better understanding of who they were and what they were like.

Have students work in small groups to locate passages of dialect in the story. They can rephrase each example as they would say it. Remind students to keep the characters' dialect accurate as they work on the activities on page 128.

At Last I Kill a Buffalo

Chief Luther Standing Bear

Selection Summary

Chief Luther Standing Bear recalls his first and only buffalo hunt. For a young Lakota Sioux boy, the first buffalo hunt was an event greatly anticipated because it was a test of manhood. During the hunt, Standing Bear is separated from the other hunters, and he kills a buffalo. Embarrassed that he needed five arrows, Standing Bear is tempted to lie about how many arrows he used. He cannot lie, and for the rest of his life, he is more proud that he told the truth than he is of killing the buffalo.

Prereading

1. Discuss Native Americans by asking students to share what they know about various peoples, customs, and ways of life.

2. Ask a student to read the introduction on page 129 aloud. Discuss what students think the selection will be about.

Active Reading

1. Have volunteers read the first two paragraphs aloud. Ask students to predict what they think will happen on the buffalo hunt and why they think as they do.

2. To maintain the oral storytelling tradition, have students prepare for and take turns reading the selection aloud.

3. Have students read the questions on page 141 silently and think about the answers.

Reading Follow-up

Discuss the questions on page 141 with the class. Elicit the following concepts:

• A boy's first buffalo hunt is an initiation into manhood in the Sioux culture.

• Because the Sioux people's lives are so dependent upon nature and the creatures that they share the plains with, they develop a deep knowledge and understanding of many animals.

• Luther Standing Bear and his Sioux peers value bravery, honesty, cooperation, honor, and modesty.

Reading Comprehension

Sequence

When an account of an incident involves many interrelated events, understanding the correct sequence of events is crucial to understanding the overall meaning of the selection.

Sequence is the order in which events happen or the order in which the author describes them. Remind students that words such as *first, second, next, before, after, then,* and *finally* are signal words that help writers present a series of events in logical progression and help readers understand the sequence of events.

Have students create a sequence chart by listing Standing Bear's actions during the hunt.

Writing

Writer's Craft: Autobiography

An autobiography is the story of someone's life written by him or her. Autobiographies not only describe the life of the author, but also the historical period in which the author lived. Have students discuss what historical information is presented in "At Last I Kill a Buffalo."

Point out that since an autobiography is written in the first person, it can include many examples of what the subject actually felt or said—unlike a biography. Ask students to locate passages in which Standing Bear reveals his emotions.

Have students keep sequence in an autobiography in mind as they work on the writing activities on page 141.

In Response to Executive Order 9066

Dwight Okita

Poem Summary

The speaker, a fourteen-year-old girl, writes a letter to an unknown government bureaucrat in response to the U.S. government's decision to imprison all Americans of Japanese descent in relocation camps during World War II. She describes herself and talks about her best friend. The letter reveals that the speaker is just like other fourteen-year-old American girls—but with a Japanese name.

Prereading

1. Ask these questions. Then discuss what it means to be an American.
   - *Why are some people distrustful of people of other races?*
   - *What makes a person an American?*

2. Have a student read the introduction on page 142 aloud. Encourage students to discuss what the poem will be about, and help them set a purpose for reading.

Active Reading

1. Give students time to read the poem silently. Then have students take turns reading it aloud.

2. Have students read the questions on page 144 silently and think about the answers.

Reading Follow-up

Discuss the questions on page 144 with the class. Bring out the following concepts:

- The speaker is a typical fourteen-year-old girl, with the same interests, problems, and concerns that girls her age experience.

- The speaker is upset with her best friend Denise because of what Denise said about giving secrets away to the enemy. The speaker simply gives Denise tomato seeds because she doesn't know what else to say or do.

- The speaker and Denise are best friends, so they must have a lot in common. They go to the same school and have classes together, and they share an interest in boys. They differ only in that the speaker is of Japanese descent and Denise is of Irish descent.

Reading Comprehension

Background Information

In December 1941, Japanese forces bombed U.S. military installations at Pearl Harbor, throwing the United States into World War II. In 1942, the U.S. government, acting on racial fears and suspicions, rounded up virtually the entire Japanese American population of the West Coast and imprisoned them in relocation camps. Despite the fact that the FBI had already arrested individuals it considered security risks, nearly 110,000 American citizens of Japanese descent lost their liberty and, in most cases, their private property. In 1988, more than forty years after the end of the war, the United States government officially apologized to the Japanese American community and made reparation to those who were relocated during the war.

Writing

Writer's Craft: Characterization

Ask students to discuss why they think the poet provides so many detailed descriptions of the speaker. Students should see that by portraying the speaker as a typical American girl, the imprisonment of Japanese Americans is made all the more tragic.

Explain that poets and authors reveal character through actions, thoughts, speech (dialogue), and direct descriptions. Have students locate lines in the poem that reveal the speaker's personality and identify the lines as actions, thoughts, speech, or direct descriptions.

Have students focus on how to reveal character as they work on the activities on page 144.

Around Brick Walls

Sarah Delany

Selection Summary

Centenarian Sarah Delany describes with relish how she foiled the bureaucracy and became the first African American teacher in an all-white high school.

Prereading

1. Ask these questions. Then start a discussion about students' experience with prejudice.
   - *What can you learn from knowing people of different races, religions, and cultures?*
   - *What can you do to fight prejudice?*

2. Have a student read the title on page 145 aloud. What do bricks and brick walls symbolize to students? Help them set a purpose for reading.

Active Reading

1. Have volunteers read the first two paragraphs aloud. Then ask students to list words that describe the type of person Sarah Delany is.

2. Give students time to read the selection silently.

3. Then have students read the questions on page 149 silently and think about the answers.

Reading Follow-up

Discuss the questions on page 149 with the class. Bring out the following concepts:

- Delany pretends there is a mix-up and skips her face-to-face interview, sending a letter instead. Then she shows up for the first day of classes, too late for the board to transfer her.

- Delany is proud of her heritage and "absolutely comfortable with" who she is. Though she has been the victim of prejudice, she has not become embittered by it.

- Delany's white colleague is surprised that Delany doesn't try to pass for white because Delany has very light skin. The colleague assumes that Delany would "want" to forsake her African American heritage to make life easier for herself.

Reading Comprehension

Author's Viewpoint

Have students describe Delany's feelings about how she was treated during her teaching career. Ask what information they used to form their opinions. Explain that Delany's viewpoint about her experiences is quite evident in her writing.

An author's viewpoint is the perspective he or she takes when writing a selection. Viewpoint can be a result of a political preference, an attitude, a belief, or a feeling about a topic or issue. A writer's viewpoint is not necessarily good or bad; rather, it simply reflects the writer's feelings or beliefs.

Have students identify parts of the story that show Delany's viewpoint.

Writing

Author's Craft: Interviews

Remind students that an interview has a specific purpose: to gather information. Therefore, it is more structured than a conversation. A good interviewer researches his or her subject and then formulates questions to ask. Questions should be simple and direct, yet contain enough information to require a specific response.

A good interviewer is a good listener who shows an interest in what the interviewee has to say. Mention to students that an interview should be well documented, either by taking careful notes during the interview or by tape-recording it.

Have students remember these points as they work on the writing activities on page 149.

Theme Links: American History

Using the Theme Links

Remind the class that the activities on these pages will help them make connections between the selections they have just read and discussed and their own lives.

All students should participate in a group discussion of the theme and complete the The Theme and You activity. Let students choose one of the remaining Theme Link activities, or encourage them to suggest other activities they would like to work on independently or with a partner or group.

Student Activities

Group Discussion
Encourage participants to list additional questions or concepts they would like to discuss. Allow fifteen to twenty minutes for the discussions. Then have groups share their observations with the class.

Imaginary Conversation
Suggest that students review the letters written by Sullivan Ballou and Sharon Lane to gather information for their conversation. Students may find it helpful to script all or part of the conversations.

Creating a Time Capsule
Encourage students to consider their time capsule objects very carefully. The time capsule should represent the students and society accurately and not simply show passing fads or unimportant information

The Theme and You
Help students see that everyone is a part of history and that each of us has a personal history. Encourage students to share their writing with the class if they wish to do so.

Checking Theme Goals

Have students refer to the goals they set at the beginning of this unit. Discuss their goals and outcomes with the class. Ask what events they might add to the timeline they worked on before reading the unit.